Architect's
Essentials of
Marketing

Other Titles in the Architect's Essentials of Professional Practice Series:

Architect's Essentials of Ownership Transition
Peter Piven with William Mandel

Architect's Essentials of Cost Management
Michael Dell'Isola

Architect's Essentials of Contract Negotiation
Ava Abramowitz

Architect's Essentials of Presentation Skills
David Greusel

Architect's Essentials of Starting a Design Firm
Peter Piven and Bradford Perkins

Architect's Essentials of Winning Proposals
Frank A. Stasiowski

Architect's Essentials of Professional Development
Jean R. Valence

Architect's Essentials of Marketing

David Koren

WILEY

John Wiley & Sons, Inc.

Library of Congress Cataloging-in-Publication Data:

Koren, David
  Architect's essentials of marketing / by David Koren.
    p. cm.
  Includes bibliographical references and index.
  ISBN 0-471-46364-7 (pbk.)
  1. Architectural services marketing—United States. I. Title.
  NA1996.K67 2005
  720′.68′8—dc22

                                        2004011437

Printed in the United States of America
10 9 8 7 6 5 4 3 2 1

Contents

Part III:
Marketing Tools and Resources:
Your Arsenal of Marketing
Weapons   191

Acknowledgments

The author would like to warmly thank the following individuals for their support, guidance, and insight throughout the process of developing this book: Meredith Berman, Carolyn Bligh, Joseph Brancato, Margaret Cummins, John Czarnecki, Joseph Demkin, Jason Hackett, Sally A. Handley, Allison Hecht, T. Kent Hikida, Jill Jordan, Lyn Hogan, Sasha Kurtz, Christina Gilson Leahy, Maxinne Leighton, Katherine Meeker-Cohen, Raheli Salkin Millman, Christey L. Robinson, Claire Schiffman, Kirsten Sibilia, Richard Staub, Natalie Wessel, Sharyn Yorio.

Introduction

I Don't Really Have to Do This, Do I?

You sell for a living. Whether you are a sole practitioner, an architect in a large firm, or a behind-the-scenes marketer, you're involved in the process of keeping your existing clients happy and attracting new clients to your firm. That's marketing, and everybody in the firm plays a part, from the receptionist to the president.

If this seems obvious to you, you're already ahead of the pack. Many architects see marketing as somebody else's job, believing that the firm's principals or their professional marketing staff bring in the work and that all the architect has to do is complete it.

Even if you accept the fact that a portion of what you do is marketing, your role in the marketing process is probably much larger than you realize. Everything you do that a client or prospective client sees or is influenced by—from a memo to your contracts to the way you present yourself—will influence how you and your firm are perceived. Ultimately, the perception of you and your firm in your client's mind is what keeps the work coming and enables you to win new work.

As a professional, you're responsible for more than just the specific duties in your job description, and your success is based on more than your expertise in your specific discipline and how well you do your job. To be truly successful in your professional career, you need to understand and serve your business. Marketing is an essential and inescapable part of business. You can't simply delegate marketing to others in your firm and trust that the work will keep coming. You need to understand how you and your firm bring in work, and you need to take an active role in the process if you're going to be in control of your career. It stands to reason that professionals who bring in work have much greater influence over the work that they do, and the overall shape of their destiny as professionals.

The Essentials of Marketing: Why the Need for This Book?

You can calm down now. Stop hyperventilating. Marketing may be your job, but it isn't your whole job. It probably isn't even a majority of your job. It's a part of what you do—ideally, a part of everything you do.

The purpose of this book is to provide a single clear source of basic marketing information for architects. There are books on marketing services and books on marketing in the A/E/C industry (many good ones are listed in the Bibliography), but this is the only book that specifically addresses the marketing needs of architects.

Architectural marketing is a relatively new concept. In 1909, the American Institute of Architects (AIA), in a "Circular of Advice Relative to Principles of Professional Practice and the Canons of Ethics," barred architects from advertising, giving away ser-

TIP

Architects who bring in work generally have much more control over the work that they get to do and the shape of their professional careers.

vices for free, or competing on fee. Architecture, from 1909 until 1972 (when the AIA agreed not to restrict its members from submitting competitive bids), was a profession that did not market itself, similar in some ways to the medical and legal professions.

Over the years since 1972, the architectural profession has changed significantly, and marketing has become an acknowledged and essential part of every architectural practice. But, as far as it has come, architectural marketing hasn't evolved to the point at which there exists a clear body of literature about how to do it; nor are there obvious places that people who want to improve their knowledge and skills can go for education. By describing the process clearly and discussing a number of the key tools, this book can hopefully help demystify marketing for architects and build a common knowledge of how architects bring in work.

The Lifeblood of the Firm: It Isn't the PowerPoint

People sometimes say things like, "Marketing is important. Marketing is the lifeblood of our firm." Is it really? Is marketing really the most important thing about your firm, the core of what you do, your "lifeblood?" It is if you work for a marketing firm, but that's a different book from this one. You work for (or own) an architecture firm. The lifeblood of an architecture firm is—drum roll, please—architecture. You aren't marketing for the sake of marketing. You aren't marketing because it's fun (though it can be). You're marketing because it's the way to meet your company's goals and your own aspirations for personal growth. You're marketing because you have a vision for where you want to go, and that vision relies on bringing in new, exciting projects and building your portfolio.

Any discussion of marketing has to begin with your vision of where you want to go personally and professionally. Marketing is a pattern of attitudes and behaviors that, if followed correctly, can help you make your dreams come true. Marketing is a tool, a means to an end, but not an end in itself. If you believe marketing is your lifeblood, step back and ask yourself, "Where am I trying to go? What am I trying to sell?" Your lifeblood is your work. Marketing is just a means to help you get more work. If you're looking for a metaphor, marketing is less lifeblood and more like "the force" from *Star Wars*. It's an energy that binds your firm together and that can enable you to accomplish superhuman feats.

REMINDER

Marketing is a process, not a product.

Design Is Different: It's Not Like Other Services

Marketing a design firm isn't quite like anything else. Though it's related to marketing construction or engineering or project management services, and it's a distant cousin of marketing other professional services like law or accounting, marketing architecture is different.

In marketing architecture, there is an opportunity to inspire and engage clients on a far deeper level than in engineering or construction or accounting or law. Architecture is about transforming the world, one building at a time, one room at a time. You're trying to change the world for the better. If your vision for how to improve your client's world complements his or her personal vision, you can connect with your client on a very deep level. At that point, you're not competing on fee or experience. You're competing on vision. Though the profession has grown up considerably (this book can stand as evidence), architecture is still an art. Architecture still has the opportunity to inspire—both in its execution (when you walk into a fantastic room, for example) and in its process (when you work collaboratively on a design with a client). It's magic. Most people can't do what an architect can, and so will stare at you in amazement while you sketch a building or an interior. When you think about it this way, it's preposterous to imagine that you may be competing on fee for a new building or a new interior. All architects will not deliver the same result. Why do clients so often seem to purchase design services as a commodity, as if all firms were the same and the lowest bidder was just as good as the highest bidder?

One reason that clients select architects based on fee is that it's really hard to comparatively evaluate vision. It's far easier to compare hard numbers. It's easy to see the difference between 100 and 90, even if the difference is only 10 percent. It's much harder to evaluate people, much harder to tell if the architect you're meeting with is the right person to help you fulfill your vision.

REMINDER

It's tough for a client to compare your vision to your competitor's. It's far easier to compare your fees.

Your Services: What Are You Selling?

One of the first rules of marketing is to consider carefully what your clients are interested in buying, and then to position what you're selling as the response to their needs. Whether the client is planning to build a high-rise office building or a house, what they're interested in buying from an architect is time and expertise. They want to hire you and your brain to help them solve a problem, to get something done. They're buying your expertise.

Architecture is a service. Marketing architecture is about promoting that service to clients who have a need for it. It's easy to fall into the trap of believing that architecture is a product, that a client or prospective client is just buying a building, for example. Or that they're just buying your portfolio. People don't purchase services the same way they buy a stereo or a television or a car. Even though many cars look alike, it's much harder to tell architects apart than it is to tell a Ford from a Chrysler. A product can be bought on past performance, based on the product's rating in *Consumer Reports.* The decision to hire one architect over another can be based only on the future promise of success, the client's belief in how you'll perform.

Because what your client is buying is your expertise, differentiating yourself from your competition happens on an individual and personal level, not from a billboard by the side of road, not from your brochure. It's easy to believe that the client's purchasing decision is rational, that the client will hire the firm that has the best balance of experience, capabilities, and fee. The fact is that the client is a person or a group of people, and who they hire will likely be based on "softer," more human factors, as well. Clients hire architects they like and trust, architects they believe will be good to work with and will help them achieve their desired results.

In this process, your portfolio of prior work is important, but it's probably less important than you think. The client isn't buying your portfolio, and

TIP

Architects, like plumbers or doctors, are hired for their knowledge and expertise.

TIP

The decision to hire one architect over another is personal. Clients hire architects they like and trust.

your portfolio isn't what you're selling. Your portfolio gets you in the game and establishes credibility, letting the client know that you've done this kind of work before, that you're capable. From there, the client will make a personal decision whether to work with you or with one of your competitors. Your portfolio, your qualifications, and your bid go to reinforce and justify the purchase decision, but they aren't the reason for it. Your qualifications and your fee enable the client to say, "See, this is why I hired this firm: They've done it before and their fee was the lowest." But it's a mistake to believe that these are the only reasons or the most important ones. Clients hire people they like and trust. And very often the client hires the people they know best.

Client Retention: It Isn't All about Proposals

It is far easier to maintain an existing relationship than to start a new one from scratch. If you're working for a client and you're doing a good job, why wouldn't the client hire you again for the next job? Why would they give somebody else an opportunity when they already know you and trust you?

Still, most marketing efforts are focused on attracting new clients, on meeting new people, building the network, and winning new work. But it's actually far more difficult to win new clients than most people imagine.

When an architect hears about a new project for a new client, he or she often imagines a fair contest between firms that is based on qualifications and fee. There must be a way to break in there, since the architect's firm has great experience and will provide

 TIP

Think of your current clients as investments. If you take care of them, they'll provide you with ongoing work, both by hiring you for future projects and by spreading the word about you to others they know.

a competitive fee. But if the client has a solid relationship with the firm they worked with on their last project, why would the client want to work with your firm? How can you differentiate yourself? It's an uphill battle, if it's possible at all. There are, of course, certain times when you'll have more of a chance to break in than others. If a client's current architect has performed poorly or lost a key staff member, for example. Or if the client has given a significant amount of work to their current architect and needs to "spread it around." Or if they're trying something new and different with their new project and want a fresh approach.

Keep your existing clients happy. That's the best marketing advice of all. Don't try to win work at the expense of the relationships you already have. Build on what you have. A bird in the hand is worth two in the bush.

The Value of Relationships

- ► Proposal: $5,000

- ► Presentation: $10,000

- ► Having a relationship with the client: *priceless*

When you have an opportunity to try to win work from a new client, you probably imagine that the prospective client is going to consider the options carefully and select the architecture firm that best meets their needs. This is generally what happens, but how the client determines which firm best meets their needs is not a straightforward process.

A client is going to hire a firm that they like and trust, on both a personal and professional level. So what makes a prospective client like and trust you?

How do you take control of this process and build a relationship?

A business relationship is like any relationship. It takes time to develop, and there are some people you're just naturally going to have more success with than others. Here are a few tips on how to build relationships with clients (or anybody, for that matter):

> *Start early.* Don't wait until there's a request for proposal (RFP) or a public solicitation. By the time the project has hit the street, the prospective client already has established connections with other firms and you're going to have a hard time building a relationship.

> *Be a human being.* Probably the hardest thing for many people to do in building a business relationship is to be truly sincere. Don't be afraid to care about the client or prospective client. Make it personal. Really care about them and their issues.

> *Listen.* Hear what they're saying. Ask questions. Don't talk so much. It's a fact: People like people who listen to what they say. You'll have time to get your point across. There's no rush.

> *Use your opportunities wisely.* Think ahead. The most natural way to meet a prospective client is to have somebody introduce you at an event. Don't squander those opportunities. If you've met somebody and made an impression, he or she will remember you when you call.

> *Connect.* Find things in common. What interests do you share? What sports do you play? Where did you go to school? What do your kids do? Commonalities and connection are where all relationships start.

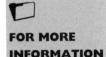

FOR MORE INFORMATION
A lot of books have been written about how to build relationships (and you can find them in both the business and self-help sections of your bookstore), most successfully Dale Carnegie's classic *How to Win Friends and Influence People* (New York: Simon & Schuster, 1936).

- *Be generous.* Give it away. Not your work and not the project. But if you've got information that might be helpful to the prospective client in some way (either personally, professionally, or for the project), give it to them. As one marketing-savvy architect used to say, "Knowledge is the information age equivalent of love."

- *Be consistent.* Don't build a relationship for one project and then abandon it. A relationship should always be about more than one project. A prospective client who may not have a project right now (or who didn't hire you for the project at hand) may have an opportunity to recommend you to somebody else for another project.

- *Don't screw up.* Your reputation is your "brand." When your name pops into people's heads, what do you want them to think? One big mistake, such as messing up on a project or mishandling your professional relationship, can be disastrous in terms of how you and your firm are regarded.

- *If you do screw up, fix it.* Things happen. Mistakes are made. What happens right after you make a mistake is critical. If you make a mistake, admit it, apologize for it, and make it right. Don't point fingers or shirk responsibility.

You're probably thinking, "This is all obvious! It's just common sense!" That's true, but it's astonishing how few people have actually integrated these behaviors into their professional lives. We all know what to do, but we don't all do it.

A Place for Passion: Big Ideas Need Big Emotions

One of the most exciting things about marketing architecture, as opposed to marketing other kinds of services, is that passion plays such an important role in the process. Because what you're selling is the promise of future performance, and your own abilities to deliver, your enthusiasm for a project can make all the difference in the world. Passion won't often make up for a total lack of experience, but in a close race between competitors who are perceived to be roughly equal, where neither has a tightly sealed relationship, your enthusiasm can put you over the edge.

That said, your excitement about the opportunities that a new project presents must be tempered. Nobody wants to work with somebody who is over-eager. One master of business development never uses the word "excited." He thinks it sounds desperate—as if he were twitching to do the project. He's enthusiastic, he's committed, he's quick to pick up the phone and make a call, to do whatever it takes to express to the prospective client the depth of his interest, but he's never excited.

Passion is personal. Each person shows his or her interest and enthusiasm differently. It may be perfectly natural for you to say, "I'm really excited about this." Or perhaps not. But you need to find ways to show prospective clients how much you want to do their projects. Your passion doesn't need to be explained or justified, as long as it's proportionate to the project. In other words, if the project is small and not terribly exciting, the passion of, "We really want to work with you!" may be all you can muster. Figure out why you really want to do this project and then express that to the client.

The Secrets of Marketing Revealed—Or Not

This book does not contain the "secrets of marketing." There are no secrets. It's all common sense. Marketing is a way of thinking. It's integrating what makes your business successful with the work you do every day, and getting your message out there.

It may seem ridiculous to say this in the introduction to a book about marketing, but marketing can't be learned from a book. There are no "10 commandments" of marketing architecture. There are no hard-and-fast rules, no independently verifiable, empirically tested formulas for marketing success. Marketing design is an extremely slippery business, because it's all about the relationships between people. There is no single road map. All the trappings of marketing (proposals, presentations, qualifications packages, brochures, Web sites, etc.) are just communication tools that help build familiarity with your firm: You have to use them to compete, but they aren't what gets you hired.

The purpose of this book is to explain how marketing works and what the basic rules are. The first part of the book talks about marketing strategy: how you plan where you want to go and put systems in place to get there. The second part describes the business development process in detail, from the initial contact with a prospective client to closing the deal. The third part reviews some of the key tools that architecture firms use to market, from brochures to technology to marketing staff.

But as comprehensive as this book attempts to be, all the knowledge in here won't "make" you a better marketer. You've got to make yourself a better marketer by improving your skills at building relationships. What this book will do is show you how the process works, so you can get into the game.

Marketing Strategy
Start at the Start

"Marketing is not a department. It is your business."
—Harry Beckwith, *Selling the Invisible*

Part I

Many architects make the mistake of thinking that marketing has only a peripheral relationship to what their firm does. In fact, marketing works best when it is totally integrated into the operations of your firm, when it's a part of everything you do.

You can't create a plan for how to improve your marketing and increase your business without first considering your long-term goals—not just in terms of fee revenue or winning work, but in terms of who you want to be and where you want to go, both as a firm and as a professional.

There are a number of ways strategic planning can help your firm:

- ► Build a shared vision for the firm's future.

- ► Articulate your vision so that it can be communicated to others.

- ► Get approval and support for the vision from senior leadership and, ultimately, your entire staff.

- ► Create a framework for all future decision making.

- ► Figure out (and agree on) how much you're going to spend on marketing and other initiatives to make it happen.

The discussion of strategic planning and marketing planning are divided into the following five areas, each with its own chapter in this book:

Chapter 1—Strategic Planning: Getting to the Starting Line

- Where do we want to go?
- Who do we want to be?

Chapter 2—Branding: We Used to Call It Reputation

- What do we want people to think of when they think of our firm?

Chapter 3—Positioning: Finding Your Place in Your Markets

- What kind of work do we want to do?
- How do we position ourselves to get it?

Chapter 4—Marketing Planning: Deciding How to Communicate to Your Markets

- What does a yearly marketing plan contain?

Chapter 5—Budgeting: Knowing What You Can Spend

- How much should we spend on marketing?
- How do we plan and track our expenditures?

Clearly, strategic marketing planning on this level can be a challenge, and many firms avoid doing it, or consider only some of these issues, or involve only some of the key players in the process. The mind-set is often, "We know who we are and where we want to go. We don't need to talk about those things. We just need to bring in more work!" But for a marketing plan to be successful, it has to start with an understanding of the firm's vision and direction. The process of defining the firm's vision and direction has to be shared by all the senior leaders in the firm, in order to get their input and approval. It can't be delegated. If the leaders don't understand it or believe in it, how can they possibly serve the plan?

Marketing Strategy: Start at the Start

Strategic Planning
Getting to the Starting Line

Strategic planning is the process of developing a vision of who you are as a firm and what your long-term goals are. It's about more than just marketing; it can influence everything: human resources, finance, information technology, operations, hiring, promotions strategy, design process, client relationships, the design of your office, and absolutely anything else that affects your firm and its performance. Firms typically engage in strategic planning at defining moments in their practice, when the firm's leadership changes or when the practice undergoes some kind of profound transformation. The strategic planning process enables the firm's leadership to build a shared vision for the firm's future, articulate the vision so that it can be communicated, and create a framework for all future decision making. When you're ready to engage in strategic planning, it's important to open your mind as much as possible. Get ready to think big.

Because strategic planning is a *process*, not a document or a report, it isn't effective for a small group of leaders to issue a fat document as the strategic plan for the firm. It will probably go unread. It will certainly not achieve approval and support from the people who need to understand it and act on it. Strategic planning is best conducted as an open process, one that involves all your firm's key leaders.

To begin the process, set up a strategic planning meeting, either as a retreat outside the office or as an extended in-house meeting. (You may want to bring in a marketing consultant to help you with this.) Figure out who should be there to give input to the vision for your firm's future. Keep the group as small as possible, but don't leave anyone out. Ask everyone to commit half a day for the meeting (two hours just isn't enough), and to come relaxed and prepared to focus on the firm's strategic direction.

Give everyone an agenda in advance and ask each person to bring historical data based on his or her area of expertise or interest (financial data, hiring or retention info, win/loss reports, client feedback, etc.). Gather any existing documents that attempt to define the firm or its vision, such as mission statements, a firm description, marketing materials, articles that have been written about the firm, and so on.

Plan to spend about half the meeting talking about where you are now (your firm, your markets, your competitors, etc.) and the other half talking about where you'd like to go (your mission, your vision, the action plan). Your agenda for the meeting could look something like this:

Strategic Planning Meeting Sample Agenda

1. Who are we?

   ➤ What makes us who we are?

2. What markets do we serve?

   ➤ Who are our clients? What are we good at?

3. What are our strengths?

   ➤ What's special about us? What makes us great?

4. What are our weaknesses?

   ➤ What could we do better?

5. What are our opportunities?

   ➤ How can we grow?

6. What threats do we face?

   ➤ What scares us?

7. What's our vision for the firm?

   ➤ Who do we want to be?

8. What's our mission?

   ➤ What do we want to change?

9. What are our goals?

   ➤ How are we going to achieve them?

10. How do we communicate the results of this meeting:

    ➤ to our staff?

    ➤ to our clients and prospective clients?

TIP

Questions are good for getting the conversation started. Keep your questions open-ended. Yes-or-no questions don't further the discussion.

Notice that these agenda items are all questions. Questions are effective conversation-starters, because they require an answer. Questions like this also convey a certain level of openness. It's not a trick, or rhetorical. The answers really are unknown, and the purpose of your meeting is to find them.

Think carefully about how to facilitate this meeting and how to capture the ideas that people have. Use flip charts to write down the things that people say so that they're recorded and so that everyone in the meeting can see them, process them, and respond to them. Let everybody know that you'll be recording the meeting in this way, and will distribute notes to them within a day or two of the meeting.

Remember that the strategic planning meeting isn't about looking smart or showing that everything's fine just the way it is. You want to create a new vision together, and it must be based on honesty and trust. Make everybody feel comfortable, appreciated, and a part of the process. Ask a lot of questions. Ask stupid questions. Listen carefully to the answers. Discuss them, record them, and learn from them.

Who Are We? What Kind of Firm Do We Have?

First things first: It's important that your key leaders are in agreement about who you are as a firm and what you stand for. It may seem simple, but the most fundamental issues are sometimes the hardest to agree on. Who are you? What are you all about?

It's not easy to frame a broad discussion like this or to determine beforehand what the answers to these questions are going to be; you have to stumble upon them. Just be as honest as possible. You're not trying to build a marketing case or define how your clients see you—that comes later. At first, you're only trying to determine how you see yourself as a firm and how you explain what you're all about.

You may want to start by asking each person in the room to say how he or she describes the firm to friends or colleagues (*not* to clients or prospective clients—you don't want to know how they sell the firm, but how they think of it). As they talk, write a few key words on your flip chart as they come up. The flip chart then becomes the documentation of the discussion—the closest thing you have to the real identity of the firm.

Once everybody has had a chance to speak, you may want to ask, "Does everybody agree with what's up here on the flip chart?" Then discuss whatever seems "meaty" or interesting, making additional notes along the way.

In some cases, a discussion like this could go on for quite some time. Within the framework of a half-day strategic planning session, set a limit for this discussion (half an hour or an hour) and then summarize. It's okay if you don't get to a "final answer" in this session. Identity is a complex issue. It may not be easy to find a neat and tidy definition of "who we are" that sounds right to everyone in the group. Expect differences of opinion. Don't ignore them; face them openly and try to integrate them and find the common threads between them.

In your discussion, feel free to mention other firms as models or benchmarks. "We're like Big Firm A, but we're smaller and more focused." "We're like Small Design Firm B, but our design style is more driven by the client than our own tastes." These comparisons help you to categorize your firm and to figure out where you fit within the solar system of your competitors.

An *identity map* is a great tool for deciding how you compare with your competitors. Select two factors, and map one on the *X*-axis and one on the *Y*-axis. (The example in Figure 1.1 uses size and a design/ specialty firm as the two factors.) Put your competitors on the map and put your own firm on the map. (In the example here, the given firms are placed more or less randomly on the map; this is not to be construed as any kind of statement about these firms.)

TIP

You may need to establish time limits for discussing each question. Otherwise, you may not make it through the entire agenda.

RULE OF THUMB

Expect differences of opinion. Try to find common ground between differing opinions.

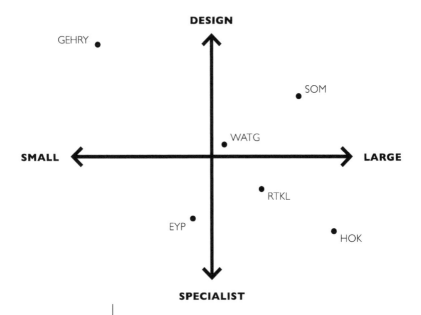

IDENTITY MAP

DESIGN

GEHRY

SOM

WATG

SMALL ← → **LARGE**

RTKL

EYP

HOK

SPECIALIST

Recognize that there are different categories of architecture firms, and that you probably fit into one of them. There are a number of ways to define the categories, but for the purpose of this discussion, let's say that there are three major categories:

► Design firms
► Specialist firms
► Large firms/matrix organizations

In the discussion of what your firm is really all about, don't be afraid to be personal, even a little bit selfish. Unless your firm is a sole proprietorship, or is strongly led by one principal visionary, everyone in the room should have a say. The vision for the firm should be the *shared* vision of the entire group. It should reflect their passions and the things that are most important to them.

Defining the Categories: Where Do You Fit In?

Design Firms

- ▶ Generally have a recognizable design style.
- ▶ Usually led by a single signature designer.
- ▶ Clients come to them because they're looking for high-impact design.
- ▶ Compete on the strength of their overall design portfolio rather than on their specific experience with a given project type.

Specialist Firms

- ▶ Can make the claim that they are the experts in one (or more) discipline, facility type, or industry.
- ▶ Clients come to them because they're looking for a high level of experience in a given area.
- ▶ Compete on the strength of their specific experience and their deep knowledge of the specific project type or industry.

Large Firms/Matrix Organizations

- ▶ Have expertise in many different disciplines, facility types, or industries, spread over multiple offices.
- ▶ May be internally structured by either practice or office.
- ▶ May compete on the basis of expertise, resources, and/or geographic reach.
- ▶ Culture, competitive advantage, work styles, and so on may be different from practice to practice or from office to office.

The strategic planning meeting will be more effective if people are comfortable talking about their passions, what's personally important to them for the firm. The questions "Who are we?" and "What are we all about?" shouldn't be addressed lightly, nor without a little soul searching. The answer needs to represent a firm that everybody in the room is proud to work for.

But this big-picture definition of who the firm is needs to be balanced with a healthy dose of realism.

Acknowledge the reality of your firm's business in light of the discussion you're having. Do your financial, human resources, and marketing efforts truly serve who you are? For example, if you're a firm that professes to be all about design, but most of your revenue comes from projects that don't include much opportunity for design, there may be an incongruity between your aspirations and your practice that you'll want to address later in the session.

Which Markets Do We Serve? Who Are Our Clients? What Are We Good At?

Next, define your markets. Markets can be defined by geography, service, client industry, and facility type. Members of one firm could define its market by saying, "We provide architectural and interior design services for academic clients in the Midwest, with a special emphasis on dormitory projects."

Title a page for each parameter: Geographic Reach, Services We Provide, Client Industry, and Facility Type. With your group's help, list the markets you serve on each sheet. Be careful to focus on the markets you work in now—not the markets you'd like to expand into (see the "Our Markets" sidebar).

Look at the listing you've made. What does it tell you? Are you highly diverse? Do you have a strong market niche? Where are the areas for investment and growth? Are there new areas you'd like to move into?

Looking at the "market map" you've created, are there key areas in which you are clearly the leader? Are there markets that you believe that you serve better than anyone else? Build a consensus from your plan-

Our Markets (Example)

Geographic Reach	Services We Provide	Client Industries	Facility Types
New England	Architectural Design	Academic	Offices
Mid-Atlantic States	Interior Design	Government	Classroom Buildings
Midwest	Master Planning	Aerospace	Warehouses
		Pharmaceuticals	Production Labs
		Chemicals	Research Labs
			Dormitories

ning group of which markets are core to your practice and which markets you're just entering.

Consider your competitors. Who are your key competitors in each market? Are there competitors that are truly formidable across the board? Are you coming up against the same key competitors all the time? Make a list of your key competitors, and briefly discuss the strengths or weaknesses of each.

Rule of Thumb:
Generalization versus Specialization

There are real advantages and disadvantages to the strategies of being either a firm in diverse markets or a niche specialist. A strategy of *generalization,* of pursuing work in diverse markets, can enable your firm to grow through pursuing new kinds of work, and is generally more stable, as the downturns in one market may be offset by the upswings in others. A strategy of *specialization,* of pursuing work in very few markets, while not usually enabling the kind of growth or stability of the generalist strategy, can be incredibly profitable. If you "own" a market—that is, you're the obvious leader—you need to invest a lot less time and money in bringing in new work, and your profitability can soar.

SWOT Analysis: Start from Now

Once you have a shared understanding of who you are as a firm and what you do, you can begin to dig a little bit deeper with a classic *SWOT analysis*, standing for *strengths, weaknesses, opportunities, threats.*

The SWOT analysis is a time-honored business tool used to assess a company's current situation both internally and externally, with a view toward developing a plan for the future. That said, the SWOT analysis is somewhat misnamed, in that it isn't really particularly analytical. It's a tool for capturing your beliefs and perceptions about your firm and the context in which you're functioning to paint a picture of your current situation. It helps you see where you are, where you could go, what you need to fix, and what you should watch out for.

Divide a piece of paper into four quadrants, and label these Strengths (upper left-hand), Weaknesses (lower left-hand), Opportunities (upper right-hand), and Threats (lower right-hand). The left side of your paper (Strengths and Weaknesses) is internal, issues within your company that you believe are either strengths or weaknesses. The right side (Opportunities and Threats) are both focused outside: What are the opportunities out there that you can take advantage of, and what are the threats that you need to watch out for?

TIP

Have a "lightning round" in which each person in the room contributes one issue to the SWOT diagram. Do it as quickly as possible to force out whatever is on the top of each person's mind.

What Are Our Strengths? What's Special about Our Firm?

Start with your strengths. What is truly special about you? Here are a few general possibilities to get you thinking, in the rough categories of design, service, and knowledge that you offer to your clients:

- Design
  - Distinctive style
  - Recognition
  - Innovation
- Service
  - Responsiveness
  - Communication
  - Speed
- Knowledge
  - Expertise in a given market
  - Specific body of knowledge (foreign building codes, etc.)
  - Relationships with key consultants, contractors, suppliers

These are only a few ideas. Brainstorm with your planning group until you come up with a list of strengths that feels complete to you.

Bear in mind that most of your competitors can probably also claim the majority of strengths that are on your list, so focus on those that are truly unique to your firm or those that are easily quantified or proved. Saying "We're responsive to clients" isn't really a useful strength, unless you can back it up with a few killer examples.

What Are Our Weaknesses? What Could We Do Better?

Be honest about this. What are the things that you don't do as well as you think you should? What are your liabilities? You may need to coax the group to be forthcoming; this isn't the time to be gentle or polite.

List everything that might affect your firm's performance, or the perception of your firm's performance, both internally and externally. Here are a few areas for discussion, and questions to get you started:

1. Design
   - ▶ Is it as good as it could be? If not, why?
2. Experience
   - ▶ Do we have enough experience in all our markets?
3. Staff
   - ▶ Do we have the right staff mix for our firm?
4. Process
   - ▶ Is our design process fluid?
   - ▶ Does everyone understand it and their part in it?
5. Human Resources
   - ▶ How is our turnover?
   - ▶ How is our recruiting?
   - ▶ How are our employee communications?
   - ▶ How is our promotions strategy?
6. Marketing
   - ▶ Are we satisfied with our marketing efforts?
   - ▶ Are we happy with our marketing staff?
7. Finance
   - ▶ Is our accounting system as efficient as it could be?
   - ▶ What about our collections?
8. Risk Management
   - ▶ Are we reviewing our contracts carefully?
   - ▶ Are we agreeing to terms that we shouldn't?
9. Recent Events
   - ▶ Has anything happened recently (staff departure, bad PR, lawsuit) that might affect our performance?

Again, this is just a list to start you thinking. Your weaknesses are what you and the group think they are. Acknowledge and record them in the meeting so that everybody can start thinking outside of the meeting about what they can do to fix them.

What Are Our Opportunities? How Can We Grow?

Opportunities are external to your firm. Looking at your markets, what are the opportunities either for growth into new markets or for developing greater depth in your existing markets? Are there trends in your markets that you can capitalize on to achieve growth?

Here are a few questions to get you started:

➤ What are the broad social or economic trends that we can take advantage of (people moving into/out of the cities, growth of assisted-living facilities, reuse of military facilities, etc.)?

➤ Are there any recent project wins or current projects that open a new market for us?

➤ Are there opportunities for convergence between our markets (for example, mixed-use facilities combining office, residential, and entertainment facilities)?

➤ Do we have any new relationships that can be leveraged to provide increased opportunity?

➤ Is there any new legislation that may affect our markets? Are there any new or proposed government spending programs?

➤ Are there any issues with any of our competitors (lawsuits, problems on projects, leadership transition) that may be opportunities for us?

REMINDER

Opportunities are external. Strengths are internal.

Keep the discussion focused on your markets (or markets you'd like to move into) and the opportunities within them.

What Threatens Us? What Scares Us?

It's easy to talk about positive things (strengths and opportunities); and if you're honest with yourself and each other, you can also grapple with issues close to you that might be negative (weaknesses). But it's very difficult to talk about those issues that are *negative* and *external*—the threats to your business. This is the most conceptual of the four areas, and the group may not have the same perception of what the real threats are. In fact, each member of your group may see totally different threats. All you can do is raise the question, start the conversation, and record the results.

Here are a few questions to get you started:

➤ Are there any broad social or political trends that may affect our business negatively?

➤ Is the business of architecture changing in our markets (for example, through the increased role of owner's representatives in the process)?

➤ Are any of our markets shrinking or drying up?

➤ Are our fees being forced down by intense competition?

➤ Are we losing a lot of work to one particular competitor?

If you can be honest about the threats you're facing, this information will be invaluable to you in choosing your future direction.

What's the Plan? Where Do We Go from Here?

So now what? You've defined who you are as a firm, what your markets are, and what your strengths, weaknesses, opportunities, and threats are. It's time to make a plan, one that enables you to capitalize on your strengths, mitigate (or remediate) your weaknesses, take advantage of the opportunities in each of your markets, and respond to (or eliminate) the threats you're facing in each market.

The plan requires three things: a *vision statement*, a *mission statement*, and an *action plan* that outlines your goals and how you propose to achieve them. The vision and the mission are related, and complementary. The vision is a statement of what the firm aspires to be, while the mission guides the direction of the action that comes out of the strategic planning meeting. The vision is an internal and, possibly, external tool. The mission is a statement that is only for internal discussion.

Business consultant Herb Cannon describes the difference between vision and mission in terms of trying to assemble a jigsaw puzzle: the vision is the picture; your mission is to complete it.

What's Our Vision for the Firm? Who Do We Truly Want to Be?

Think big. Okay, now think bigger. The vision statement is the place to use superlatives: best, leading, largest, most, finest. In your wildest fantasies, what is your firm all about? Design? Innovation? Efficiency? Service? How do you improve the lives of your clients? How does your firm change the world for the better with every project you complete?

AT HAND

The vision and mission are complementary statements that guide your firm's actions. Your vision is a statement of who you aspire to be as a firm. Your mission is a summary of your plan of attack.

A vision statement could be something like this:

AB&C is a design firm that improves the lives of hospital patients and medical professionals by taking a fresh look at healthcare design and applying the best practices from around the world to our projects.

Clearly, you could go on and on, especially if you're active in many markets. Try to say it as concisely as possible. Write it out first, then cut things that aren't critical or that only support your main idea. See if you can get it down to one key idea. Make it as active as possible; use active verbs. Here's a better one:

DE&F designs the most successful hotel and resort properties in the world.

It can be very challenging to write a statement like this in a group. You may not get to your final answer in the session, but try anyway. Begin with a blank piece of paper. Ask the group to throw out words that describe what they think the firm is, at heart, all about—not the realistic, earthbound stuff, but the truly aspirational and inspirational. How do you impact the world?

Once the ideas start rolling, you'll be able to see which rise to the top. And after you've accumulated enough raw material, prompt the group to pick what they think the absolutely most important things are; then take a pass at writing down the vision statement. Ask the group to edit it. Move on when you feel that you've accomplished all you can in the meeting. You may need to rework it after the meeting before you send it out for the group to review.

What's Our Mission? What Do We Want to Change?

A mission statement is much more directed than the vision statement. It describes not who you are, but where you're going. It describes how you plan to change the company—not the world. Think big, but create a mission that is within the bounds of reason. The mission statement should be followed by an action plan that describes exactly how you will achieve the mission. Here's a sample mission statement:

> *We intend to transform our company into the most respected laboratory design firm on the West Coast. We will accomplish this by hiring the best staff, rigorously improving the quality and accuracy of our design, and delivering on our promises.*

Start developing your mission statement by asking the question, "Where do we want to go now?" Is there a market that you'd like to dominate? Is there an area of your practice that you'd like to improve? Be as specific as possible. This is a mission: It needs to be focused. Look at your weaknesses and threats from the SWOT analysis. What is it that you want to fix? What is it that you'd like to improve in order to truly fulfill your vision? Look at the opportunities, as well. What current trends or changes in your markets can you take advantage of to transform your company for the better?

Just as with the vision statement, recognize that you may not be able to complete the mission statement while you're in the meeting. Everybody may need to give it some thought. Let it go when you feel that you've gone as far as you can. Remember that what's most important isn't the final product of a neat and tidy plan, but the process of working together with the key minds in your firm to get there.

What Are Our Goals? How Are We Going to Achieve Them?

The goals come directly from everything you've talked about so far. What did the SWOT analysis indicate that you should work on? In which markets are you the strongest? The weakest? Think about how each area of your practice supports your mission, and develop goals for each area:

➤ Design

➤ Technical

➤ Management

➤ Human Resources

➤ Finance

➤ Legal

➤ Marketing

➤ Office Operations

➤ Other

Each goal should have an action plan that accompanies it. For example, under legal, you may have a goal like, "Update our standard contract language." The action plan might be something like this:

1. Check what the latest AIA contracts are.
2. Find our what other firms are using for standard contracts.
3. Review what contract terms clients have asked us to agree to lately.
4. Talk to our lawyer.
5. Revise standard contract.

Because of the detailed nature of the action plan, it may be difficult to develop this fully in your group.

You may want to agree on the goals in the meeting and then assign someone from the meeting to develop the action plan in each area.

Before you adjourn the meeting, set a date for a follow-up meeting in a few weeks or a month later. Indicate that you will distribute notes from the meeting. These notes are, essentially, a rough draft of your strategic plan.

Strategic planning is an ongoing process. In the next meeting, you'll need to revise the action plan and make sure it represents everything you must do to fulfill your mission. Check back at a quarterly meeting to make sure that you're on track: that the vision statement still reflects your aspirations, that the mission statement still reflects the direction you're moving in, that the action plan is still valid, and that you're making progress.

How Do We Communicate the Plan to Our Staff? To Our Clients and Prospective Clients?

As noted earlier, a strategic plan isn't a fat, bound volume that sits on your shelf, unread. It should be a concise and *living* document that reflects who you are, where you're going, and what you propose to do to get there.

As soon as possible after the meeting, compile all of your notes into a document. The organization for the document could be something like this:

1. Who We Are
2. Our Markets
3. Strengths, Weaknesses, Opportunities, Threats
4. Our Vision

TIP

Don't let it die. Once you've revised your action plan and you have a strategic plan, check back at a quarterly meeting to make sure that you're on track.

TIP

Don't let your notes from the meeting sit on your desk. Compile them immediately after the meeting while they're fresh in your mind.

5. Our Mission
6. Action Plan

While you're compiling, feel free to edit and fill in the blanks to make this a more complete document. Circulate this document to all of the attendees at the meeting, asking for comments. If it's appropriate, supplement the action plan with supporting materials (a draft marketing plan for target markets, for example, or a detailed financial analysis). In your follow-up meeting a few weeks or a month later, validate the strategic planning document and discuss how to share it with the other members of your firm.

If you've got a culture that supports it, share the entire revised strategic planning document with your firm. Or, if there's sensitive information in the document, share an edited version. You may want to take out the SWOT analysis, for example, and edit the detailed action plan down to just a set of goals. But keep in mind that the more of the plan you share, the greater understanding there will be at all levels of the organization, and the more support

---

Old Vision, Old Future

One firm went through a strategic planning initiative at the highest levels, and invested a great deal of time and resources in the process, but unfortunately failed to communicate it down to the staff level. The only evidence of change to the average member of the staff was a new internal and external marketing slogan: "Bold Vision, Bold Future," which was posted on the wall and inserted in marketing materials. But the new slogan (and the mysterious new bold vision) didn't have support from the staff, because they didn't *share* the vision. How could they? It had never been communicated to them. And so the new slogan became something of a joke. "Old Vision, Old Future," one staff member quipped while walking by the giant slogan in the hallway.

you'll be able to earn to make the strategic changes that fulfill your mission.

One word of caution: The strategic plan is not a marketing tool. There is very limited value in sharing any of the information (except, perhaps, the vision statement) with clients, prospective clients, or anybody outside your firm. The strategic plan is a product of the collective soul-searching of your firm. It should inform all of your actions and communications, but it doesn't need to be shared with anyone outside your organization. It's for internal use only.

Branding
We Used to Call It Reputation

2

"Products are made in the factory, but brands are created in the mind."

—WALTER LANDOR

We all know what branding means in the world of products. Think of a few great product brands—Sony, Nike, Mercedes, IBM, and Volvo: We associate these names with brand attributes or even marketing slogans, such as safety for Volvo, or "Just Do It" for Nike. In many cases, these brands evoke an emotional response. You feel like you know these companies and their products. They're like old friends.

Brands are an incredibly effective means of communication. If a company is branded clearly and consistently, customers will have a sense of what to expect, and will associate the company with certain key ideas. Many people believe, for example, that when they buy a Sony product, they're getting something that is reliable, efficient, and well designed. Companies with strong brands occupy a certain space in the customer's mind, and it's very difficult for another company to replace them. IBM means business computing, and though Intel,

REMINDER

People attach personal meaning to brands.

Microsoft, and Dell each occupies its own corner of our minds, none comes close to knocking IBM out of position or taking away its association with business computing.

Why are brands so effective? Because we're overloaded. We are subjected to far more communication in any given day than we can possibly process. Advertising is ubiquitous—on television, on the Internet, in the mail, in the newspaper, on billboards. In order to make sense of the confusion, our minds attach meaning to symbols and names. We look for signs we can trust so that decisions are easier to make. Product companies have recognized this and have been taking advantage of this for years, tailoring their messages through advertising to try to carve out space in our minds for their products.

The idea that a services company has a brand in the same way that a products company does is, however, relatively new. Professionals such as doctors, lawyers, accountants, and architects have historically relied on their reputations to build their businesses, not on advertising or brand-building. If they did good work, their clients would spread the word and the professional's reputation would grow.

Times have changed. Word of mouth by itself is too slow a communications medium. You're competing in a global marketplace, for projects outside of your local area against firms from other parts of the country or the world. You still submit proposals, but you wonder whether anybody reads them anymore. You go on interviews and you wonder whether the decision was made before you walked into the room. The point is, you need every advantage you can get to differentiate yourself from the competition, as early as possible in the decision process. You need to be in the client's mind before the request for proposal (RFP) is issued. You need a brand.

Your brand is an extension of your reputation. When you think of architects like Frank Gehry, Richard Meier, or Cesar Pelli, certain associations pop into your head. These architects have strong reputations and, therefore, strong brands. What about large architecture practices like SOM, HOK, and Gensler? Clearly, it's a little more complex due to the size, breadth, and reach of these firms. But if you practice architecture or work in the design professions, each of these names means something (or a package of somethings) to you.

TIP

Do everything you can to set yourself apart from the competition. Your brand can help make the differences clear.

There's a quaint resistance to branding that many architecture firms share. They believe that if they do good work, if they build the better mousetrap (or design the better building), the world will beat a path to their door. But, in a world where you can choose from 15 different kinds of mousetraps, how do you tell them apart? How do you assess which is better, and for which application? Well, you read the label, of course, and you look for a brand that you can trust.

The line between products and services is getting fuzzier all the time. Products are becoming more like services and services more like products. Just about everything you buy today, whether sugar from the grocery store or help with your tax return, is some combination of product and service. The difference is in the mix. Companies have learned that they can gain a competitive advantage by adding service to their products or stressing the tangible results of their services.

Think about the leading brands that you encounter every day—brands like Dell, McDonald's, Federal Express. Dell is a computer company, but its reputation is based on service, on the reliability of its computers and the on-site service its workforce provides. McDonald's is the fast-food leader, but it's the experience of buying and consuming its food that brings people back, not just the food itself. Federal Express is all service—a heavily branded delivery service specializing in overnight delivery. Dell is probably 80 percent product/20 percent service; McDonald's is around 60 percent product/40 percent service; and Federal Express is 5 percent product (the tracking slips, the packaging, the box on your desk, etc.) and 95 percent service.

TIP

Architects can take some lessons in branding from large corporations.

What about your business? What's the product/ service mix in architecture? Even though you're principally providing a service, the eventual result of your collaboration with a contractor and others is a product: a new or renovated building or environment. So, is architecture 75 percent service and 25 percent product? Whatever the mix, it's clear that products and services are not as mutually exclusive as we once thought, and professionals who provide services can take some lessons from product companies that have been building brands for years.

Why Do You Need a Brand? Because You Already Have One

When your clients or prospective clients hear your name, what do you think pops into their heads? High design? Attentive service? A specific design style? A specific project? If you're Frank Gehry, it's probably the Guggenheim Museum in Bilbao.

These associations with your name and your firm are your brand. You don't have a choice in the matter. If people know anything at all about your firm, they'll have an impression of who you are and what you're about. They'll file these impressions in their heads for easy recall when somebody mentions your firm's name.

You can't control what people remember or what people think of you. But you can influence it. If you decide on a specific brand message for your firm, you may be able to convey it to your audiences in a way they'll remember. What comes to mind when you think of Federal Express? Chances are it's the slogan, "When it absolutely, positively has to be there overnight." Federal Express spent a lot of time and money to get that message into the public's head, but the result is inestimable in value. It's the company that most people think of when they think of overnight delivery, consequently it owns a majority of that market.

Clearly, it isn't feasible for architecture firms to spend millions a year on advertising and brand-building like the Fortune 500. Luckily, you don't have to. You build your brand with every interaction that people have with your company or your work, whether they call you on the phone, work with you in person, visit your Web site, leaf through your brochure, or live or work in one of your projects.

The consistency of their experiences with you and your work builds your brand—that is, the impression of you that your audiences (clients, the press, the public, etc.) have in their minds. It's a very powerful force if it's used effectively. If you say that you're all about service, and everything you do and everything that people see supports this, they'll remember it. You'll become known for service, provided you deliver on your promise.

There are three enormous advantages that companies with clear brands have over those without

BRIGHT IDEA
Word association: List some architects and try to summarize their brand or reputation.

RULE OF THUMB
You build your brand with every interaction.

clear brands: recognition, focus, and trust. Here's the meaning of each:

- *Recognition.* People can identify you. Example: "Look! The Golden Arches!"
- *Focus.* People know what you do and can easily associate your name with that concept. Example: "It has to be there overnight, so I'll use FedEx."
- *Trust.* People know what to expect from you and they're confident investing in you. Example: "It'll work; it's a Sony."

If your prospective clients recognize your firm, understand your focus, and know that they can trust you to deliver on your promises, you will have an unbelievable advantage over your competition. Two architectural precedents are Richard Meier and HOK Sport+Venue+Event (an independent division of HOK).

When you think of Richard Meier, you think of white. Most of his firm's work is white, his Web site is white, and his office is white. His work is recognizable; we know his focus and we know what to expect. Critics might say that his work is always the same, but the strength of Richard Meier's brand is in the consistency of his work and its presentation. Your impressions of the quality of the work are secondary; whether you're an ardent Richard Meier fan or not, you know his work and you know his brand.

HOK Sport+Venue+Event is the unchallenged leader in the design of sports arenas. This firm has worked for most of the major baseball and football teams in the United States and has designed arenas around the world. Its name alone gives them a claim in the sports and arena market, and the work of their designers backs that up. Anyone creating a new sports arena would no doubt call them. Which is not to say they would automatically be selected, but that they would be first in the minds of many because of the brand they've built through their firm name and their work. The name points out how specific their focus is: These are specialists, and it's easy to believe that they know what they're talking about.

Building a successful brand is about finding your message and reinforcing that message consistently in every contact you have with your audience. Your message follows directly from your vision statement. If your vision is to be the premier laboratory design firm in the world, your message might be one of technical expertise. If your vision is to be a firm that designs entertainment venues, your message might be that you're exciting and flashy. Think about who you want to be and then write down the simple messages you'd like to communicate through your brand.

What's in a Name? Rise Above the Alphabet Soup

One of the most important tools in brand communication is your firm's name. Unless you're just starting your practice, you probably have a name for your firm already. But it's important to think about the significance your name has to people who hear it, and how it supports your vision and your brand.

Many architecture firms have names that began as the combined surnames of the partners. Often, for some reason, there are three partners: Hellmuth, Obata & Kassabaum; Skidmore, Owings & Merrill; Looney Ricks Kiss; Kohn Pedersen Fox. Sometimes it's four names and sometimes it's two, but

RULE OF THUMB

Build your brand by determining your message and supporting it in all of your professional interactions.

REMINDER

In crafting your message, start with your vision statement. Think about who you want to be and create simple messages that reinforce this vision.

frequently it seems to be three. When these long firm names become shorthanded to acronyms, we get HOK, SOM, LRK, and KPF. Unless you're very familiar with these firms, this starts to sound like alphabet soup. Who got that project? Was it BBB or BBG? Was it IA or AI?

The best names are distinctive and memorable, and that's tough to do with a bunch of letters. People remember names and words much more easily than an apparently random group of letters. Names and words have traction in the mind.

Basically, there are three types of names for architecture firms:

> *Multiple proper names.* Difficult to remember, and usually shortened to acronyms. Examples: HOK, SOM, LRK, HLW, KPF, BBB, BBG, WATG, P&W.

> *Single name of signature architect or company founder.* Generally calls up the image of one visionary. Examples: Polshek, Gensler, Jerde, Rockwell.

Avoiding Pitfalls: Naming Tips

> *Avoid acronyms.* Acronyms (usually formed from a set of proper names) are difficult to remember and are confusing, leading to alphabet soup: HOK, SOM, LRK, HLW, KPF, BBB, BBG, WATG, P&W, and so on.

> *Make it unique.* Was it Pei Cobb Freed or the Pei Partnership? Perkins & Will or Perkins Eastman? AI or IA? Pick a name that doesn't sound like another firm's name.

> *Give it relevance to what you do.* Is there any ambiguity about what HOK Sport+Venue+Event's key markets are? Putting your specialty right up front makes your focus crystal clear.

> *Don't be generic.* The name Interior Architects (IA) certainly describes what they do, but little else. People remember names that are distinctive.

► *Anything other than a person's name.* Less ego implied, but can also seem less personal. Examples: Studios, Morphosis, Pentagram.

Whatever your firm's name, think about it carefully. Consider both how it looks on paper and how it sounds when people say it. Is it easy to spell? Is it easy to say? Will it be clear to somebody who doesn't know you how to pronounce the name? Consider any connotations that the name has in your mind and the mind of your audience. Does it sound like anything else? Do you have an emotional response to it? Does it sound like the firm you want to be? If it's a person's name or one combined from several surnames, what connotation do those family names give you?

Building Your Brand: Communicating Who You Are to the World

Let's say you know who you are as a firm and what you stand for. You've got a clear vision, and you've decided what you want people to know about you. How do you use your brand to communicate with your audiences?

Example: A Great Name

Pentagram is a great company name. Principally a graphic design and branding firm, Pentagram provides architecture as one of its services. It's a great name because it's the word for a geometric symbol with five sides and five points, representing the fact that the firm had five founding partners; and, as graphic designers, geometry is their business. Thus, the name implies a symbol that represents both what they do and (if you know the story) how they started. There's a lot of communication packed into that three-syllable word.

Who Are Your Audiences?

First, define the audiences you're trying to reach. These aren't just clients. To influence the way you're perceived, you need to think about all the different groups that may have impression of who you are and what you're all about:

- ➤ Clients
- ➤ Prospective clients
- ➤ Employees
- ➤ Prospective employees
- ➤ The industry (consultants, contractors, suppliers, etc.)
- ➤ The competition
- ➤ The media (reporters and critics)
- ➤ Academia
- ➤ The general public

Where Are You Starting From?

Consider where you are right now. What do people think of you? How do you think you're perceived now? What does your name mean to your audiences? Are there any liabilities or difficulties with these perceptions?

To gain an understanding of how you're perceived, do a little research. Ask your audiences what they think of you. Take a client or an owner's representative or a friend in the industry to lunch, and ask him or her frankly what he or she thinks your firm's strengths and weaknesses are. Listen very carefully to everything he or she says.

What's the Message?

What do you want to say? What do you want your audiences to know about you? Again, your message should be a direct reflection of your vision statement. Keep it as simple and clear as possible, or it may be difficult to communicate (and be received) effectively.

What Are the Points of Contact?

Think about every contact that your audiences have with your firm. Every contact should express and reinforce your message. Here's a short list:

- ► Your work (built, unbuilt, documents, etc.)
- ► Your people (on projects, your receptionist, mailroom staff, etc.)
- ► Word of mouth (what other people say about you)
- ► Media and press coverage
- ► Your logo and signage
- ► Your office
- ► Business cards
- ► Direct mail
- ► Advertising
- ► Proposals
- ► Brochures
- ► Presentation materials

Later chapters will cover producing communications materials that reflect and reinforce your brand. The most important (and most difficult) place to reflect your brand message is in the people who work in your firm.

Your People Are Your Brand: Everybody Has a Stake in It

You're a service firm. You're selling and providing services to your clients. Services are provided by people. It is absolutely critical that your people reflect your brand message. The people in your firm are the most tangible contact that the world has with your company. Everything else—logos, brochures, proposals, whatever—is secondary, and derivative. If your people don't believe it, it isn't real.

The power of your brand reflected in your people cannot be overstated. Think about brands that are known for exceptional service, like Disney or Nordstrom. Companies like this have long since recognized the power of getting their employees to believe in their message. If you don't have your people on board, they can undermine and invalidate any attempt to position your brand. If you say you're the world's preeminent entertainment design firm but your people don't believe it, watch out. A McDonald's ad campaign a few years ago was, "We love to see you smile." I don't think the staff of my local McDonald's cared whether I smiled or not. The McDonald's message was totally disconnected from my experience in my local restaurant, and the message started to seem silly.

It is vital that your people believe in your firm and its message. How do you get them there?

> *Believe it yourself.* If the leaders of your firm don't believe in your message, there's very little chance of communicating it.

> *Be truly passionate about it.* Your enthusiasm will convince others. Care about the message (and spreading it) and others will follow your example.

- *Share it with them.* Be frank and open with your people about your brand and your message. It's their brand, too. It's their identity as well as yours.

- *Give them a part to play.* Make it clear to your people what you expect from them—how they should represent the firm and what the key messages are. Make sure they know that you're all in it together.

- *Reinforce it with action and repetition.* It isn't enough to say it once. Back it up with investment and action. Let your people see that you mean it. And keep repeating and reinforcing the message.

- *Encourage two-way communication.* If there's a perceived inconsistency, if your people don't believe what you're saying, it's better to find out sooner rather than later so you can correct it. Foster an open environment where people are comfortable saying what they think. Truly listen to what they have to say.

Living Your Brand: Walk the Talk

Whatever you do, you must continue to back up your brand with results. A brand is empty and hollow if it's not consistent with the service you provide and the quality of your work. A good brand helps communicate the quality and value of your services to your clients, prospective clients, and other audiences. A good brand can't take the place of good work. Your brand has to reflect who you truly are and what your honest aspirations are. If you're fibbing, your staff will know, and before long your clients will, too. Keep it real, and continue to back it up by delivering on your promises.

Positioning
Finding Your Place in Your Markets

3

Branding and positioning are two sides of the same coin. Your brand is how your firm is perceived by your audiences; branding is the process of trying to influence their perception. Positioning is the process of packaging your company for a specific target market and determining how you define your firm relative to your competition in that market. Branding and positioning go hand in hand. Your brand will imply your positioning, and your positioning will influence your brand.

The key difference between branding and positioning is in scale and focus. Your brand applies to your entire firm, in all markets, and should originate from your firm's vision statement. Your position applies to one market only: How do your present yourself to this market and differentiate yourself from the competition?

Like branding, positioning is an ongoing strategic process. But the value of your position in a market becomes most apparent when you're planning the pursuit of a specific opportunity. Your position is where you're starting from, what your clients think of you before they open your proposal or grant you an interview. What do clients know about you? What

Example: The Rockwell Group

The Rockwell Group is an example that illustrates the difference between positioning and brand. Though Rockwell is thought of by many to be *positioned* as the leader in restaurant design, the Rockwell Group's *brand* is about the "wow factor" of its projects. The Rockwell Group has worked on hotels, retail environments, theater sets, casinos, and even a children's hospital—not just places for food, but places where "wow" design makes an impact on visitors.

do they think of your work? How are you positioned in this market? Are you the leader? The underdog? A newcomer?

For many architecture firms, the marketing process begins when they receive an RFP. They read about the project and think, "Sure, we can do this project," and submit a proposal. They don't consider how they're positioned in the market, or how winning this project would help improve their positioning, or even why they really want this project. Unless a firm already has a very strong relationship with the client, they probably lose. They're capable of doing the work, but they haven't made a compelling argument why they're the right choice. They haven't figured out their positioning in this market or for this project.

"We can do it!" is not a compelling positioning, unless you're proposing to do something nobody else can do (like build a space station on Mars or complete a project in a ridiculously short time frame). You're competing in a highly competitive marketplace. If all you've got is the basic capability to do the work, you will probably lose to firms that offer more—firms with expertise or additional capabilities that you don't have. You have to position your firm in this way: "We can do it better than anybody else, because . . ." Answer the question: What makes you the best choice for this project and other projects in this market?

When you receive an RFP or hear about a new project, you need to evaluate the opportunity in terms of how it fits into your strategic plan and how you are positioned in the market. At that point, the relationships that you have are absolutely critical, but they're not enough on their own. You need to assess and utilize your positioning. In fact, your relationships with people involved in the project can help establish and verify your positioning. You can ask those in the know, "Would you consider our firm for something like this?" Or, "Did you know that we specialize in this project type? We've done many similar projects. Do you think we would be considered for this project?"

In order to be successfully positioned in a specific market:

> *You need to stand out.* You have to be perceived as unique among your competitors.

> *You have to focus.* You can't be "all things to all people." You have to demonstrate that you have specific knowledge and a specific perspective.

> *You have to back up your words.* Empty claims and promises won't get you far. Be very specific as to why you are the right choice.

Clearly, in an extremely competitive market, it's going to be tough to stand out. What makes you truly unique (and not just "uniquely qualified" as so many proposal cover letters claim)? How do you build a position for your firm?

Leaders and Followers: Getting to the Top of the Ladder

One of the first questions to think about is whether you want to position yourself as a leader or a follower in your market. There are real advantages to being the leader: You're associated with the market (when people think of designing a hotel, they think of WATG), and you can usually charge higher fees than the competition. So how do you get to be a leader?

In their landmark marketing book *Positioning: The Battle for Your Mind* (McGraw-Hill, 2001), Al Ries and Jack Trout claim that people create associations and "positions" in their minds for things because we're simply overwhelmed with too much information and trying desperately to organize it in some way. Ries and Trout describe positioning in terms of ladders in the audience's mind: Each ladder is a market. Each rung is a brand. Where a brand fits on the ladder is its positioning. Imagine what the positioning ladder looks like for cola drinks. Rung 1: Coca-Cola. Rung 2: Pepsi-Cola. Rung 3: RC Cola. Rung 4: Everybody else. Once the ladder is set in the mind, it's very tough to improve your positioning and move up the ladder. Even though Pepsi generally wins in blind taste tests, it can't knock Coke out of its position. If you're competing in the sports arena market against HOK Sport+Venue+Event, you may be able to beat the firm on one project, but it's going to be very difficult to knock it off the top rung of the ladder. It's probably going to be the first firm that your client or prospective client thinks of when they think "sports arena design," and there's not a whole lot you can do about that.

Why is that? How did HOK Sport+Venue+ Event get on the top rung of the ladder? How do you get to be on the top rung? The easy way is to be the first one there. HOK Sport+Venue+Event was the first firm to say, "Sports arenas are what we do," and it locked that idea into our minds by making its name reflect its specialization, and by backing it up by designing a lot of sports arenas.

It's nearly impossible to get to the top of an existing and established ladder, where there's already a firm that is identified as the leader in everyone's mind. Sit back, be patient, get used to being number 2 (or 3 or 17) and wait for the firm ahead of you to die. This can take years or a truly monumental error on its part. Andersen was on the top rung of accounting before it mishandled the Enron account. Spectacular failures like this are rare, but they do happen.

So, while it's very difficult to climb an existing ladder and knock another firm off (because it's their ladder and they were there first), you can always go down to the hardware store and buy your own ladder. You can always redefine the market to suit what you do. New ladders are created all the time. Define your own market so that you're first in it!

You may not be able to overtake HOK Sport+Venue+Event's positioning in sports arenas, but what about concert and event venues? Is HOK Sport+Venue+Event on the top rung of that ladder? What about smaller sports arenas—Little League parks, high school football fields? Which firm is on the top of that ladder? What about specializing in arenas for a single sport? Is HOK Sport+Venue+Event on top for soccer fields? Maybe it is, but if you're positioned as the specialist for soccer fields, even HOK Sport+Venue+Event's highly focused positioning can start to seem broad if you're competing for a soccer field.

BRIGHT IDEA

Corner the market by defining it. Find an unclaimed niche and you can become the leader!

TIP

New ladders are created all the time.

The challenge is to define your market (your ladder) as specifically and concisely as possible so that people can accept it as a unique market, remember it, and associate your firm with it. For models, look at the architectural marketplace. How many "top rung" design firms can you name? Rockwell in restaurants, Gensler in interiors, Polshek in museums, WATG in hotels, and on and on.

Followers, in contrast, generally position themselves as the lower-cost or higher-service alternative to the leader. Followers can be very successful: Think Avis or Pepsi or Burger King. But they seldom overtake the leader. Followers need to be positioned clearly, as well. The Avis slogan, "We're number two—We try harder!" gives the company a firm placement in the mind of the customer as the higher-service alternative to Hertz, the leader in the market.

TIP

Positioning yourself as an alternative to the leader won't enable you to replace the leader, but it may secure your place as number two.

Staking Your Claim: Developing Your Positioning

The process of positioning involves a little more than just creating a new ladder and scrambling to the top of it. What type of ladder do you want to create? How do you define your market, and what do you offer it? Why should you choose this market, and how will you back up your position as leader in it?

Much as your vision statement describes what you'd like your firm to be, your positioning statement sums up your market and your position in it:

JKL is the leader in the design of intermodal transportation facilities. We [are different from the

*competition because we] have a thorough
understanding of the complex circulation issues of
people, trains, buses, and cars.*

Developing a positioning statement is a four-step process:

1. Definition: What is the market?
2. Needs assessment: What does it need?
3. Competition: Who's the competition?
4. Differentiation: What do we offer?

In each step, it's important to be as specific as possible. Generalities won't help you. In order to build a useful positioning statement, as precisely as you can, you have to define your market, its needs, and what makes you different.

What Is the Market?

The market is defined by *service*, *facility type*, *client industry*, and/or *geography*. It can be any area that you perceive as a marketable specialization and any permutation of these factors. You could, for example, determine that your market is the interior design (service) of retail locations (facility type) for fashion companies (industry) in the western United States (geography). Or that your market is real estate developers in Boston. Or laboratory projects for chemical companies around the world.

What Does It Need? What Are the Priorities in This Market?

To determine what the needs are in your market, you may need to do a little research. Talk to your clients and prospective clients. Find out what they'd like to do differently, but so far haven't been able to. Find out what their hot issues are. Find out what the trends are, what's coming down the pike, what's

RULE OF THUMB

Be as specific as possible in defining your markets.

TIP

Talk to your clients and prospective clients to try to find unsatisfied opportunities in the market.

next. Can you identify any unsatisfied opportunities in the market? Is there any need that you might be able to fulfill better than your competition? What is the "better mousetrap" that clients in this market would love to have?

Who's the Competition? What Other Firms Are Serving This Market?

In order to position yourself in the market, you've got to know whom you're up against. What other architects do work in this market? How are they perceived? What's their positioning? Is another firm the clear leader in the market? (If so, you may want to redefine the market.) Are there any weaknesses in the competition against which you may be able to define yourself? "We're just as good as RST, but we're cheaper!"

What Do We Offer? What's Different about Our Firm?

TIP

Define as clearly as you can what makes you different from your competitors.

Most important to determining your positioning is to determine what you offer to this market that none of your competitors can match. What distinguishes you from the pack? What experience, capabilities, or attributes do you bring to this market that are truly unique? Why would a prospective client in this market be foolish to hire the competition?

Writing the Positioning Statement

Once you've answered these questions, you can put it all together into a clear positioning statement, following this outline:

1. What is the market?

   ► Mini-storage facilities in the Midwest

2. What does it need?

- Speed of delivery, experience, guaranteed delivery
3. Who is the competition?
   - Big regional firms
   - Design/build firms
   - Small local firms
     (None specialize in this market)
4. What do we offer?
   - Speed, agility, specialization

Here's a one possible positioning statement:

PQR is the leader in designing mini-storage facilities in the Midwest. We can design and deliver a mini-storage facility faster than anyone.

Then you just have to spread the word in every communication you have with your market, and back up your positioning by delivering on your promise.

Choose Wisely—and Be Prepared to Live with Your Decisions!

Many firms resist positioning. A positioning implies a business strategy, implies a focus. A positioning is limiting, but the power of position far exceeds the restrictions. To be first in the mind is priceless, even if you're first in the mind for dormitory design. There are still a lot of dormitories out there.

Choose your position carefully. If you have a choice between a position that is more technical (and specialized) and one that is more general, choose the more technical. People associate. "If this firm can design a BL-4 lab for the Centers for Disease Control, it can certainly design my high school biology lab." It's a lot harder to work the other way.

Choose your positioning based on your mission. If you want to be the premiere hospitality design firm, define a part of the large hospitality market as your market (Native American gaming? boutique hotels? riverboat casinos?) and grow from there. Think about markets that have the most opportunities and position your firm to take advantage of those.

Be prepared to live with your decisions. When you respond to an RFP for a specific opportunity, work with the positioning you've built. You can't reposition your firm for every opportunity that comes up. Last week you were the expert in this, today you're the expert in that, tomorrow you're the expert in something else. You can't change the tune that fast, and it can be perceived as insincere to try. You aren't going to be the right choice for everything, so pick the specific market you want to be the leader in, and work it.

If you're like most architecture firms, you work in a lot of different markets. You may design labs and hotels and dormitories and houses. You have positions in each of your markets, and you should work on developing them and defining what it is you stand for in each. But accept the fact that you can't be the leader in all of them. This doesn't mean you should restrict yourself to the markets that you're the leader in, just that you should build your leadership position in a specific area and grow your business where you can. Focus on what's important to you and your business, and be a leader.

Avoiding Pitfalls: You Can't Be All Things to All People

Most architecture firms believe openly or tacitly that a solid positioning limits their flexibility and their appeal. "So what if we're the leader in dormitory design? We want to design hotels!" Many firms resist positioning at all for this reason. They don't want to be pigeonholed or limited in any way by how they're perceived.

A positioning as leader in a market is an incredibly valuable thing. You're in the audience's mind. The followers probably aren't, or at least don't occupy the same position.

To attempt to make your positioning broader (or to avoid having a strong positioning at all) limits its effect. Your audiences think, "Can they really be so good in dormitories if they also design hotels?" "I hear they design good dormitories, but they don't seem very focused on that."

It's better to be on the top rung of a small ladder than the bottom rung of every ladder. It's very difficult to market a jack of all trades.

Think about the big ladder: "Architecture." Where do you fit on that ladder? If you ask most Americans the name of an architect, they'll say Frank Lloyd Wright. He's been dead for 50 years and he's still sitting on the top rung in *your* industry.

Do you really think you can compete with that? Pick a smaller ladder, and own it. Then grow into other markets from your existing position.

Marketing Planning
Deciding How to Communicate to Your Markets

4

Most architecture firms aren't particularly rigorous about marketing planning. Either they've never made a plan or they have a plan that nobody pays attention to. It's a rare firm that creates a marketing plan that everybody in the firm understands, accepts, and follows.

A marketing plan is a tool to help provide structure to your marketing efforts. Where there's a plan, there's a common understanding of what the marketing goals and objectives are and what actions the firm is going to take to build its business. It's a measuring stick that guides your decision making. When any kind of opportunity arises—whether a project or publicity or joint venture—the marketing plan provides a context for evaluating the opportunity and determining how to proceed.

A marketing plan is proactive. It anticipates where you'd like to be in a year, or in five years, and lays out a process to get you there. It's about growth, not merely sustaining your current position in the market. It's tough to grow without a plan. Most firms without marketing plans consider themselves opportunistic, able to take advantage of anything that comes up. But this is a reactive approach to marketing, not a proactive one. Without a plan, you can probably win work and sustain your current client relationships, but it's going to be difficult for you to penetrate new markets or significantly increase your market share in existing markets.

Without a plan, there's no direction guiding your decisions. Each decision must be made on the spur of the moment, without the benefit of really understanding how what you're doing today will help you get to where you want tomorrow (or in a few years). There are many reasons why architecture firms avoid marketing planning, or don't take it seriously:

▸ Marketing planning is no fun. ("Not *another* meeting!")

▸ There's no pressing deadline driving the planning. ("Let's talk about that next week.")

▸ They don't want to limit their choices about projects to pursue. ("How can we know today what we might want to go after tomorrow?")

▸ There's a lack of understanding of the importance of a marketing plan. ("Why do we need a plan? Just get out there and win jobs!")

▸ There's a lack of investment in the planning process. ("If we had a plan, nobody would pay attention to it anyway!")

▸ Planning doesn't seem like an appropriate use of staff time. ("People should be working on projects, proposals, and clients, not planning!")

▸ Marketing is perceived as being a secondary activity, rather than an integral part of running the business. ("Marketing planning? We've got a business to run here!")

▸ The process of writing a marketing plan is too daunting. ("I can't be bothered.")

► They're too busy with active projects. ("I don't have time.")

Whatever the reason, and whatever the excuse, without a marketing plan, you're rudderless. You're making decisions that aren't guided by a consistent framework. You need a marketing plan so that everybody understands what the goals are, what the targets are, and how much you plan to spend to accomplish your objectives. A marketing plan also gives you a yardstick of goals and objectives to measure your success against.

What's in It? The Contents of the Marketing Plan

Depending on the size and focus of your firm, you may have a marketing plan for the whole firm or one for each targeted market. Generally, most firms should have more than one marketing plan; you're probably in more than one market—even if you only design (and are only interested in designing) a few project types, such as academic research labs and government research labs. These two markets are different and require a different strategy.

There's no magic to a marketing plan. At its simplest, the marketing plan should answer these basic questions for the market that it covers:

► Where are we now?
► What do we want to go?
► How are we going to get there?

Here's a sample table of contents for a marketing plan:

1. The Market
2. Our Mission
3. Current Position

TIP

A marketing plan should be short. Keep it to a page if possible. The longer it is, the less likely it is that anybody is going to read it.

TIP

Have a separate marketing plan for each of your markets.

4. Market Size and Trends
5. Competitors
6. Positioning
7. Objectives
8. Responsibilities
9. Schedule
10. Budget

A marketing plan should be no more than a page long, if possible. You may be thinking, "How can I get all that on one page?" Well, summarize. Make bullet points. Say it in as few words as you can. If you need two pages, it's not the end of the world, but don't write four pages for each heading! Keep it simple to make sure that the plan will be read and followed. Unlike the strategic plan, the marketing plan can be drafted by one person and distributed to other decision makers for review and approval. Just make sure they read it. Too many good marketing plans languish in inboxes, unread, while everybody goes about their business. A marketing plan is useless unless the decision makers in your firm understand it and agree to it.

Here's a short discussion of each heading and an example of what you could write:

1. *The market: Whom are we trying to reach?* Define the market as precisely as you can in terms of the four market qualifiers from Chapter 1: geography, service, industry, and type of facility.

   "Architectural design of garages for shopping centers in Florida."

2. *Our mission: What do we want to accomplish?* Describe specifically what you're trying to do. What's the major goal of this marketing plan? What do you want your position in this market to be?

"We want to be the leading designer of garages for shopping centers in Florida. We want to double our revenue in this market in the next year."

3. *Current position: Where are we starting from?* Write down where you are right now in this market. Are you a veteran, trying to regain your position, or are you a newcomer?

   "We have designed three multistory garages for shopping centers in the last year. We are thought of as a designer of garages for corporate offices, not shopping centers."

4. *Market size and trends: How big is the market? What's changing?* You've got to know your market. Can you estimate the size of the market? How many projects a year are there in this market? How profitable are they? Are there trends in this market that you can take advantage of?

   "Ten to 20 new shopping centers are built in Florida each year. In addition, older shopping centers are being reclaimed as corporate offices (5–10 last year). There may be an opportunity to leverage our corporate office parking garage experience to expertise in shopping centers."

5. *Competitors: Which firms are we competing against? What are their strengths and weaknesses?* You have to know who the competition is. Your prospective client will be comparing your credentials with those of other firms. Which are the other firms? What are you positioning yourself against?

   "VWX designs shopping centers and parking garages. RST designs parking garages and lots, mostly for sports arenas and amusement parks. CDE designs anything, anywhere."

6. *Positioning: How will we position our firm in this market?* Where do you want to stand in this market? Have you defined the market in such a way that you can be the leader in it?

   "We are the leading firm in designing parking garages for shopping centers. Unlike our competitors, we are specialists in this project type. We have deep experience in parking garage design, not only for shopping centers, but also for corporate offices."

7. *Objectives: How are we going to do it?* Break down your mission into smaller pieces. What can you do to achieve your mission? Think of your entire arsenal of marketing tools (covered in the rest of this book). How can your proposals and presentations help you? How can publicity help? Direct mail? Advertising?

   "We intend to:

   ▶ *Build our network of shopping center developers.*

   ▶ *Redesign our marketing materials.*

   ▶ *Conduct a direct mail campaign.*

   ▶ *Get articles placed in trade publications; improve our proposals.*

   ▶ *Be more aggressive in closing the deal."*

   Be as specific as you want here. If there's anywhere in the plan to add additional detail, it's in this section. This is the heart of the plan—what you intend to do to fulfill your mission.

8. *Responsibilities: Who's going to do it?* You have to name names, or everybody will think that you're going to take care of it all by yourself. If your objective is to build your network, who's going to do it? Who's going to attend more industry events, take more people to dinner, and get more introductions? Put at least one name next to every item on your objectives

list. Break up these items if you need to. "Improve our proposals," for example, is somewhat vague. Is there a graphics task, a writing task, and a procedural task, for example? Assign one person to each task. Spread around responsibility. The market leader shouldn't do it all by himself/herself. Everybody who's involved in this market should share in the responsibility of fulfilling the plan.

9. *Schedule: When will we check back?* Make it very clear in the plan when you'll check in on progress. By what date is each person named supposed to have accomplished his or her objective? Let them know the timeframe. If this is a one-year plan, you may want to check back every month or two to review progress, update the plan, and make new assignments.

   "The timeframe of this plan is one year. We will check on progress next month."

10. *Budget: How much are we going to spend?* This budget should quote a specific dollar amount for your firm's marketing efforts in this market. It should include hard costs (reproduction, printing, etc.) and soft costs (staff time). You may want to break out a few big-ticket items, such as a new brochure or attendance at a trade show, for example.

    "Our budget for the year is $20,000; $5,000 of this will be for printing new marketing materials, and the rest will be for networking and pursuing specific opportunities."

    Remember that this budget is only a guideline, an estimate to keep you on the right track. Hopefully, depending on the culture of your organization, you can adjust the budget later if a great opportunity comes up (a design competition or a trade show or a joint venture). It's important to set a realistic number to ensure that everybody is on the same page from the outset. (See the next chapter for a more in-depth discussion of marketing budgeting.)

Your Existing Clients: Where Do They Fit in the Plan?

In many firms, marketing is all about getting new projects from people they don't know. But it is much harder to convince someone you don't know to hire you than it is to convince someone you do know. As part of your planning process, consider carefully how much emphasis to place on new clients and how much to place on existing clients. The mix will vary depending on your focus, your current position in the market, and your goals. But to leave existing clients out of the plan is probably not a good idea.

REMINDER

It's much easier to hold on to your existing clients than it is to recruit new ones.

Your clients can help you in more ways than just handing you work, as well. Your existing clients make great references, and can refer their friends and business associates to you. A third-party recommendation can be incredibly valuable to building business. Your positioning is much more credible when it comes not out of your mouth, but out of the mouth of one of your clients.

Plan to nurture your relationships with your recent and existing clients. It can help you in ways that may not be directly evident, but that can have a significant payoff down the road.

Living with the Plan: Don't Let It Die!

Your marketing plan is a living document. Don't file it away! Keep it on your desk. Make notes on it.

Cross things out. Let it change as often as it needs to. Keep pushing it forward, relentlessly. You didn't go through the trouble of writing the plan to have it languish. You wrote the plan to have it acted on in order to grow your business. Writing the plan isn't the end of the process; it's the start.

Have a regular meeting to check in with everybody who is involved in the plan and building your business in the market. Schedule this meeting for every month, every week, or at whatever frequency suits the speed at which you intend to proceed. Update the plan at these meetings. Reissue the plan to the group when it's got enough scribbles on it. Put a date on the plan so everybody knows they've got the most recent version.

Over the life of the plan, things will happen. Opportunities will come up that you hadn't anticipated. You may have serious setbacks for one reason or another. Your market may change dramatically. Don't let a challenge to the plan make it obsolete or irrelevant. Meet with your group and update the plan to reflect the new conditions. Do it as soon as possible so that everybody has the same understanding of where you go from here.

When opportunities appear that you hadn't envisioned, think carefully about how you should respond. If it's an attractive opportunity, like a design competition or paid publicity, you will probably find that there are two competing visions of how to respond, either in yourself or in your planning group:

RULE OF THUMB

Use your marketing plan as a tool to evaluate new opportunities as they arise. How do they fit in the plan?

1. We can't do that! It's not in our plan!

2. It's not in our plan, but it serves our mission. We should do it!

The opportunity may not be anticipated in your plan, but it might serve your mission, the *spirit* of your plan. Use your mission as your guide. If the opportunity serves your mission, and you can afford it, let the plan change to encompass the new opportunity. If it doesn't serve your mission, or the price is too high, defer to the existing plan, full steam ahead.

In any case, accept the fact that every plan has a natural lifespan. There will come a time when your marketing plan will need to be scrapped, either because you've met all your objectives and achieved everything you had hoped to achieve or because you're leaving the market or have lost interest. Whatever the reason, let the plan go, and make a new plan.

Budgeting for Marketing
Knowing What You Can Spend

5

Without a budget, a marketing plan is just words. You need a budget to provide a financial framework for your marketing plan, defining how much you can spend in order to accomplish your objectives. A budget brings clarity to your decision making—an item is either in the budget or it isn't. When an opportunity comes up, your options are clear: Do it (because the budget allows it), don't do it (because it doesn't fit in the budget), or reevaluate the budget to see if there's a way to make it work.

Budgeting can be a difficult process. It's tough to put dollar values on expenses that haven't appeared yet and expect to live by them for the lifespan of the budget. How are you supposed to know what's going to happen in six months? How can you possibly anticipate how many award submissions you'll complete or how many presentations you'll make over the course of a year? You can't; and that's the point. That's exactly why you need a budget: so you have some guideline to determine whether an opportunity is reasonable in terms of its cost.

Ideally, you should create a marketing budget for each market you're now in or planning to enter, as well as a marketing budget for the firm as a whole.

This allows you to look closely at how much you're investing in a new or established market over time. If you find you're spending more on a specific market than you feel you should, you can shift your budget to a different market.

Many firms create marketing budgets on a yearly basis, to coincide with the firm's annual financial results and budgeting for the coming year. Choose a time frame for the budget that suits your needs. If you're planning a six-month push into a new market, you may want to prepare a specific budget for that effort and time frame.

Preparing a Budget: Throwing Numbers at the Wall

Budgeting is more art than science. If this is your first time preparing a marketing budget, your results may be rough, and you may need to adjust your budget periodically throughout the year. It's only through an annual process of looking at what was spent and adjusting your projections that you can get to a solid budget for marketing. If this is your first budget, feel free to make some assumptions and guesses. You have to start somewhere.

In order to evaluate your marketing expenditures on a market-by-market basis, you'll need to create a budget for each market you're in, as well as for your firm's overall marketing effort. One of the first tasks is deciding which line items belong to the budget for the individual market and which belong to the *overhead* of marketing your firm. It's generally easy to decide whether items like trade shows or new brochures belong to one market or to the entire firm, but what about publicity? Unless you have a public relations consultant working for you in one market only, the cost of having that consultant may need to be carried in your overall marketing budget.

Here's a list of some of the items that should go into your marketing budget, whether for your office, your firm (if you have more than one office), or for a specific market:

Soft Costs: Staff Time
- ► Principal time
- ► Staff time
- ► Marketing staff

Hard Costs: Expenses
- ► Photography
- ► Brochures
- ► Reprints
- ► Direct mail
- ► Award entries
- ► Advertising
- ► Publicity
- ► Trade shows
- ► Short-run printing: proposals, presentations, qualifications
- ► Research
- ► Travel
- ► Networking
- ► Memberships
- ► Training

You may want to create a matrix to prepare your budgets, with each of these expenditure categories down the left side and each market (or office) as columns across the top . Make sure you create a column

SAMPLE BUDGET MATRIX

SOFT COSTS: STAFF TIME	ACADEMIC	LABS	OFFICES
PRINCIPAL TIME			
STAFF TIME			
MARKETING STAFF			

HARD COSTS: EXPENSES			
PHOTOGRAPHY			
BROCHURES			
REPRINTS			
DIRECT MAIL			
AWARD ENTRIES			
PUBLICITY			
TRADE SHOWS			
SHORT-RUN PRINTING			
RESEARCH			
TRAVEL			
NETWORKING			
MEMBERSHIPS			
TRAINING			

for firmwide expenditures (not office- or market-specific) and a column for your total.

Now the guesswork begins. As you invent numbers for each category of expenditures in each market (filling in each box of your matrix), bear in mind that there are three ways to arrive at a number in each category:

1. Actually determine what you think you'll spend in each category (on a new brochure, for example).
2. Look at last year's numbers (your budget, as well as how much you spent) and adjust your budget up or down based on how much you actually spent last year and your sense of how your marketing efforts (overall or in each market) will change in the coming year.
3. Base your numbers on benchmarks from other firms that you consider comparable.

The first method (actually figuring out how much money you'll need to spend) is by far the most reliable, but some categories in your budget will defy estimation. For example, it can be tough to estimate how much money and time you're going to spend on ongoing or frequent activities, such as proposals or award submissions. It really helps if you have a prior year (the second method) as a benchmark that you can adjust based on what's going on in your markets.

The third method (basing your budget on data from other firms) can be difficult, too, in that you have to first know what comparable firms are spending on marketing. A number of consulting firms that work with architects, including Zweig-White and the Professional Services Marketing Association (PSMA), conduct surveys that give some indication of what firms spend on average. The American Institute of Architects (AIA) and the Society for Marketing Professional Services (SMPS) have also surveyed their members on budgeting and expenditures. This data may be somewhat general, in that it can give you only a sense of the average among firms rather than a comparable firm, but it can still be helpful as a rough benchmark.

Hard Costs and Soft Costs: Time Is Money, Too

The most important categories on your budget are principal time, staff time, and marketing staff. Unless you're doing a tremendous amount of printing, the vast majority of your investment in marketing (probably 75 to 80 percent of your costs) is in the time that people spend in marketing-related activities.

Some firms budget for marketing based only on hard costs (printing, reprographics, membership fees, etc.) and ignore soft costs, rolling principal time, staff time, and marketing staff costs into an overhead allocation. A marketing budget that doesn't include people's time ignores your largest single line-item expense. Printing is cheap compared to how much staff time is worth.

TIP

Track the time that people spend on marketing. You need to know how much time you're investing in each market.

You need to track the time that people spend on marketing if you want to get an accurate picture of how much you're investing in a particular market. This may involve working with your firm's accounting system to create marketing *billing codes* for tracking time that people spend on general marketing, building a specific market, or advancing a specific opportunity. Many firms have a set of billing codes for each market or activity, and create new codes when they enter a new market, receive an RFP, or begin to track a new opportunity.

It can be difficult to estimate how much time people are going to spend on an activity over the course of a year. You can throw a number at the wall (based on a few hours per week, for example), but it may not bear much resemblance to how much time people will actually spend. It's easy to say, "We'll devote 1,000 hours of time to building this market over the next year," but this number is just a guess or an arbitrary limit. It's not based on how much time you reasonably expect marketing activities to take, because it's practically impossible to determine this over the course of a year. Your best guess may be as close as you can get.

When you estimate principal and staff time, put down both the number of hours and the dollar value of those hours. It can be uncomfortable to translate someone's efforts into a specific cost, but you have you look at it as a dollar value in order to make accurate comparisons between markets and to truly understand the level of investment that you're making. A large number of hours, by itself, can seem conceptual and disconnected from the cost. What is a thousand hours worth? But a thousand hours of someone's time who makes (or bills) $50 an hour is $50,000, and that's nothing to sneeze at.

In converting principal or staff hours to a cost, you have a few choices of which dollar value to use for each person on a per-hour basis. You can use each individual's *billing rate* per hour, which is the rate that you charge your clients for the individual's time, and includes all costs to the firm, plus an allowance for profit (generally calculated by taking direct costs times a multiplier). Billing rates are higher than your firm's actual cost and may give you a budget that is disproportionately high; but depending on your

BRIGHT IDEA
Assign billing codes for different marketing opportunities and market segments.

firm's culture and policies, these numbers may be easier to get and use than actual costs. You can also use actual salary rates in your budget, but, obviously, there may be sensitivity about working with the dollar value that people actually make; and using the salary rate doesn't reflect the actual cost to the firm, as it doesn't include benefits and other costs. Ideally, depending on how your firm's accounting system works, you can use a rate per hour for each person, which includes benefits and overhead (an *actual cost*) but not profit.

In calculating the cost of principal and staff time, use the data you can get. It's better to have a rough budget than none at all. If you can't get rates per person per hour, or aren't comfortable using them in your budget, create your principal and staff time budget by category. For example, based on your firm, you might estimate that a principal's time is worth around $100 per hour, and a staff member's time is worth around $50 per hour. Plug these rough numbers into your budget and see what you get. It's not exact, but it's better than nothing. This will at least give you a relative estimate of your investment in various markets and activities that you can work with.

REMINDER

Hourly billing rates are considerably higher than your actual cost. Using billing rates in your budget will give you disproportionately high numbers. Try to use actual costs in your budget if at all possible.

Budgeting: The Big Picture—How Much Is Enough? How Much Is Too Much?

You have to be realistic about your budget, and think about how best to allocate your investment across your entire budget, in each of the markets you're in. Recognize that it probably doesn't make sense to spend the most money on promoting your firm in your biggest or most profitable markets. If you are the dominant player in a given market, you may decide to spend less on that market and more on new markets you're entering. It can take a significant marketing investment (again, materials *and* time) to enter and be taken seriously in a new market.

At the same time, you can't assume that you can neglect established markets in favor of new markets. You have to continue to invest in your strongest markets to maintain and grow your position. Your objective is different in established markets than in new markets, but you still need to make an effort and an investment.

Look at your overall budget once it's drafted and see how it is balanced between new and existing markets. Is the budget fairly allocated to markets in relation to their strategic priority for your firm? Have you allocated enough to the new markets to truly make an impact? Have you allocated enough to the established markets to continue to grow and maintain your position there?

Many firms want to know how their spending compares with that of their competitors. One major benefit of budgeting is that it provides a rough benchmark against that of the rest of the profession. As mentioned earlier, a number of consultants and organizations (Zweig-White, PSMA, AIA, SMPS) conduct surveys and publish average expenditures for marketing. The amount that firms spend on marketing varies, but most firms (large or small) seem to spend between 4 and 8 percent of their annual revenue on marketing (including time and expenditures). Firms that focus on maintaining their existing position in established markets are closer to the 4 percent end of the spectrum. The marketing budget

TIP

Think carefully about where you want to devote the most resources. It may make sense for your firm to make a bigger investment in new markets than in established ones.

gets higher based on speculation in new markets. Obviously, if you're making a big push into one or more new markets, you can expect your numbers to be much higher.

The high cost of entering new markets is the reason it is critical that your marketing budget be in alignment with your firm's strategic and marketing plans. Think about it: if you're trying to push into a market in which you don't have much experience, it can take years to break even, to reach a point where your profit from that market matches or exceeds your marketing expenses. You have to be sure you want to do it before you start spending large amounts of time and money. The value of a plan and a budget is that it enables you to make these decisions with both eyes open, and with all the decision makers in your firm in agreement.

Exceptions to the Rule: Going around and over the Budget

The fact is, many firms enter new markets accidentally. Sometimes it just happens. A great opportunity comes up, the stars are in alignment, a project is won, then another, and before you know it a new market is born. Your marketing planning and budgeting shouldn't get in the way of this natural evolution of your practice. All your plans and estimates need to be open to adapting to the changing market and to new opportunities as they come up. The budget provides a guideline, but it shouldn't be an absolute rule.

When any kind of opportunity comes up, whether a potential project or a publicity opportunity or a new relationship, you have to evaluate it carefully. Ask yourself the following questions:

1. **Is this opportunity in alignment with our mission?**
   Does it reflect who we are? Does it reflect who we want to be and how we want to be perceived?

   ► If yes, go on to question 2.

   ► If no, stop here. If it doesn't fit your mission, why do you want to do it?

2. **Is it in the plan? Does it fit the budget?**
   Does our strategic or marketing plan anticipate an opportunity like this? Do we have enough money budgeted for this?

   ► If yes, stop here and just do it.

   ► If no, go on to next the questions.

3. **What's the potential benefit?**
   Understand the total opportunity here, in every sense. Will this opportunity bring in revenue directly? Can it expose us to new markets? Can the opportunity get us closer to our vision for the firm? How badly do we want it?

4. **What's the total cost?**
   How much is this opportunity really going to cost us, in terms of time and money? Are there hidden costs? Can we limit the costs?

5. **What's the risk?**
   Is it a sure thing? What's the likelihood that our investment will bear fruit? 100 percent? 10 percent? Somewhere in the middle?

6. **Is it worth it?**
   Given the risk, is the potential benefit worth the total cost of the investment? Is this the best deal (given benefit, risk, and cost) that we can get?

   ► If yes, go for it and don't look back.

RULE OF THUMB

The budget provides a guideline, but shouldn't be an absolute rule.

> ▸ If no, pass on the opportunity but acknowledge that it was a close one—there was a real interest on your part that drove you through the evaluation process. Keep your eyes open for a better opportunity with greater potential benefit, less risk, and hopefully less overall cost.

Your budget is a living document. The reason to have a budget is to provide some shape to your decision making, not to limit you from taking advantage of opportunities as they arise. Use your budget as a measuring stick, not as a rulebook.

Keeping Track of What You Spend: Accounting and Marketing

You need to have a system in place to track expenses and principal and staff time over the life of your budget. If you're in a larger firm, you'll want to work with your accounting group to create a system for opening and tracking project numbers for each opportunity and each market. If you're in a smaller firm, you may be able to track time and expenses less formally, simply by logging into a spreadsheet the time and money people spend.

In any case, it's good to look at your time and expenses every month or so to see how they are in alignment with your budget. Did you spend more (or less) on any given activity than you had anticipated? Are there any patterns that you can see that may threaten your budget over time? Is all the principal and staff time spent on each market where you think it should be?

If you see a problem with expenditures relative to the budget, raise the issue as soon as possible, with

TIP

Think of your budget as a living, evolving document.

everybody involved. Make sure that those who worked with you on the budget, as well as those who are in control of the expenditures, understand that there's a risk of blowing the budget. It's in everyone's best interest to take the budget seriously and to try to live within it. If the budget is ignored or discarded, it will be much harder to create a new budget for the next year.

The Business Development Cycle

Getting the Job

To many architects and other professionals, "sales" is a dirty word. The idea that they would have to "sell" something makes them break out in a rash. Many people hate to sell. I hate to sell. When I think of sales, I remember going door-to-door selling hoagies or candles or holiday cards for my scout troop or to pay for a trip to Europe with the Spanish Club. I think of rejection. I think of standing in front of my neighbor's door with an order form, in the rain, begging the man or woman behind the door to consider buying some lovely candles that I've only seen in a catalog.

"Business development" has a much better ring to it than "sales." It sounds professional; it sounds like there's an established process for bringing work in. It doesn't sound weak; it doesn't sound like begging at all. It doesn't sound dishonest. It inspires confidence.

If you don't like to sell, don't. Your clients don't really want to be "sold" on you and your firm anyway. They want to be convinced. Sometimes, they want to be wooed. You'll need to be persuasive. You'll need to make a compelling case for why you're the best. You'll need to connect with the client or prospective client on a personal level. But you don't need to beg or try to sell clients something they don't need. You're a professional, and there's a professional way to build your business.

From the architect's perspective, the business development process is about convincing the pro-

TIP

Clients don't want to be "sold." They want to be convinced. Sometimes, they want to be wooed.

spective client that your firm is the best firm for the job. The conventional selection process is often conceived and explained as very straightforward and linear—that you move from hearing about a project to getting more information to presenting your qualifications, proposal, and presentation, and then, if you're the client's top choice, entering negotiations and winning the project.

THE BUSINESS DEVELOPMENT PROCESS

LEAD ▶ RESEARCH ▶ RELATIONSHIP ▶ QUALIFICATIONS ▶

▶ PROPOSAL ▶ PRESENTATION ▶ NEGOTIATIONS ▶ PROJECT AWARD

This process has evolved as a structured way for clients and their consultants (project managers, owners' representatives, real estate brokers) to rationalize their purchasing process and justify their eventual decision of one firm over others.

Instead of a straight line, we can also think of the process as a funnel: Many firms are qualified, fewer will be invited to submit a proposal, fewer still will be asked to present, and only one firm will be interviewed.

The industry and the government have supported this kind of approach to the selection of architects and engineers for years. In 1972, Congress passed the Brooks Act, making this process government policy: "The Congress hereby declares it to be the policy of the Federal Government to publicly announce all requirements for architectural and engineering services, and to negotiate contracts for architectural and

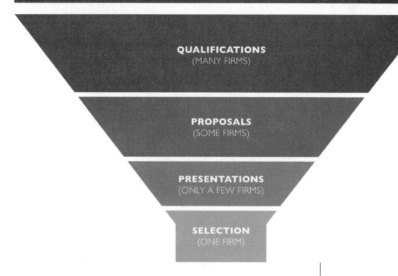

THE PURCHASING PROCESS

QUALIFICATIONS
(MANY FIRMS)

PROPOSALS
(SOME FIRMS)

PRESENTATIONS
(ONLY A FEW FIRMS)

SELECTION
(ONE FIRM)

engineering services on the basis of demonstrated competence and qualification for the type of professional services required and at fair and reasonable prices."

The intent of the Brooks Act was to institute Qualifications Based Selection (QBS) for the procurement of architecture and engineering services on the federal level, rather than allowing these services to be bought and sold purely on the basis of fee. The net result varies from agency to agency (and has been implemented to various extents on the state and local level).

Generally, the selection process for public work goes something like this:

1. *Public announcement.* The project is announced in the *Commerce Business Daily* (CBD) for federal projects, or in some other public source for state and local projects.

2. *Qualification statements.* Interested firms are invited in the announcement to submit their qualifications. Often these qualifications are to be submitted on specific forms, such as the old Standard Forms 254/255 or the new Standard Form 330. This varies by agency and by state or local government.

3. *Evaluation of qualifications/development of a short list.* The qualifications are evaluated. The number of candidate firms is narrowed down to a short list. The short list is invited to the next stage, generally either to submit technical proposals or to present for the project.

4. *Technical proposals and interviews.* Depending on the agency, locality, and specific project, short-listed firms are asked to prepare technical proposals or presentations, or sometimes both. Generally a sealed *fee proposal* is submitted with the technical proposal.

5. *Ranking of the firms.* The firms are ranked based on how well they meet the agency's criteria for this project.

6. *Negotiation with top firm.* At this point, the Brooks Act dictates that the agency should enter negotiations with the top-ranked firm. Often this means that the fee proposals (if submitted) are opened at this stage. In some cases, the agency will negotiate with the top-ranked firm, using the fee proposal as a starting point. In other cases, the low-bidding firm of the three ranked firms will be retained.

As you can see, it's still a funnel. The process provides the opportunity for any architect to see the solicitation and submit qualifications, but only a few will be invited to submit a proposal or make a presentation, and only one firm will ultimately be selected.

Every client, whether in the public or private sector, approaches the selection process differently. There are many variations on the standard selection funnel. Sometimes, if the client knows the firm they want to hire, and can get away with it without facing scrutiny from within their firm or agency, they'll enter negotiations with one firm without a selection process. (This is, of course, ideal for the firm in question.) In other cases, a qualifications presentation will come before the proposal, rather than after. Other selection processes involve design competitions so the client can "see what you can do."

In any case, though the process may seem to be structured in a straightforward and linear way, it's a mistake to think that the client's decision process is similarly straightforward and linear. The formal process exists to rationalize the client's selection process, to help explain why one firm was selected over the others. The process doesn't get you hired, but it will help to justify why your firm got hired and the other firms didn't.

Let's be honest: Though architects enter the selection process assuming in good faith that the process will be fair, the client's decision process isn't generally linear or rational at all. Clients pick firms they like, for reasons that are often difficult to describe. There is no automatic, linear process for selecting an architect. It's totally subjective.

Of course, you'll have a tremendous advantage in the process if you already have a relationship with the client—if you've worked for the client before and you're liked and trusted. The process of marketing to existing clients even has a different shape: Rather than a funnel, it's a client relationship cycle. If you view your relationship with your client as an "account"

REMINDER
Every client approaches the selection process differently.

TIP
The formal process exists to rationalize the client's selection, which is not always straightforward.

TIP
There's no automatic process for choosing an architect. The process is inherently subjective.

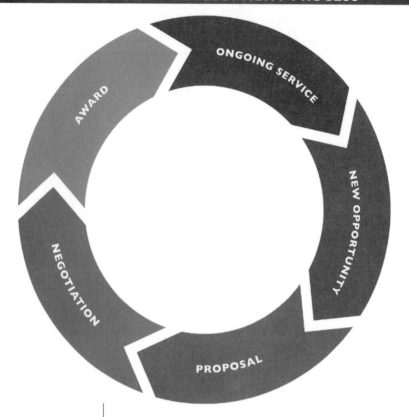

rather than on a project-by-project basis, the process is an ongoing cycle of service that leads to additional opportunities.

In this model, business development never ends. The entire cycle is about servicing the client, and through service, building your business with your client. You provide a high level of service and your client keeps coming back to you for additional projects.

Ideally, the client has such confidence in you that they can award you new projects without competition. Even if you have to compete in order to satisfy additional stakeholders (a board of directors or an agency's purchasing policies), you'll have a strong voice on the client side pulling for you. You'll be able to get more accurate information from the client and have a clearer sense of the real issues at the outset of the process. You'll have a decisive advantage against your competitors.

In fact, unless you know the client, it can be tough to tell how the process is going to unfold. What are the real issues? What's the client's vision for the project? What are the priorities? Who's the real competition? You can't assume that it's a fair contest. Even if the process is run as a typical linear selection process (qualifications, proposal, presentation, negotiations), there are a number of possible behind-the-scenes scenarios that can make it impossible for you figure out what your chances of winning are:

▶ *The client knows which firm they want to hire from the beginning.* The entire selection process is an exercise to justify the choice of a preselected firm. In this kind of contest, your firm (if it isn't the favored firm) is only a "stalking horse."

▶ *The client is a selection committee of a number of people.* There may be more than one set of issues and preferences at the table. In a private-sector project, for example, there may be competing priorities related to image, human resources, and finance. How do you present yourself as the right choice to everybody who has a vote?

▶ *The client is bottom-line-focused and is going to hire the least expensive firm no matter what.* Sometimes, unfortunately, price is truly all that matters. The client sees all firms as relative equals in terms of capability and will hire the least expensive competent firm.

RULE OF THUMB

Having an existing relationship with the client can be an invaluable help, even if you have to compete. You can get a sense of what the real issues are, and you may even have a strong voice on the client side pulling for you.

TIP

If you know the client, you can tailor the proposal to their priorities.

All you can do is to listen carefully to the client, try to figure out who they are and where they're coming from, consider their objectives and priorities carefully, and respond as best you can with your qualifications and proposal, tailored to your understanding of the client and what they're looking for.

If you don't know the client, it's important to acknowledge that there are certain projects on which the client is going to be more willing to take a risk than others. If this is the fifth similar project that a client has undertaken, and the client hired the same firm for the first four, it's going to be tough to break in, unless that firm screwed up on the last project. Conversely, if this is the first project of its kind for this client, and you're an expert in this project type, you may have more of a chance.

So what makes a client hire you? What is the purchase decision is based on? Broadly speaking, you need to have five things to get hired for almost any job: a good reputation, experience, trust, passion, and the right fee. Which factor is the most important will depend on the client, and there may be other pertinent factors for specific projects, as well. There are exceptions, of course, but most of the time, you can't get hired without all five covered:

> ► *Reputation of you and your firm (brand).* Nobody wants to hire a loser. All things being equal, it's better to be known and have prestige.

> ► *Experience.* If you haven't designed anything like this before (in one sense or another), it may be very hard to convince the client that you know what you're doing.

> ► *Trust (identification/chemistry).* A client has to trust you. The trust can come through identify-

ing with you ("I went to Penn, too!") and through building chemistry.

▶ *Passion.* You need to care about the project. If you don't care, somebody else will.

▶ *Compensation.* You need to be "in range." Sometimes you need to be lowest. In any case, you have to ask for a fee that the client considers reasonable.

These are not factors in reality as much as they are the factors in the client's mind. The client will almost always hire the firm that, in the client's perception, has the best mix of these five factors.

So, how do you influence the client's perception of you? What can you do to improve the way that you're perceived? Here are a few things that can influence perception of you and your firm:

▶ *Hearing of you before (previous relationship, word of mouth, media).* If the client knows you, or has heard of you, and has "heard good things," you're off to a great start.

▶ *Third-party endorsement.* Have an independent source (another client) rave about you to the prospective client. Include client quotes in your materials.

▶ *A promise ("added value").* If you make a promise to a prospective client in an authentic and heartfelt way, it shows that you take responsibility and that you care—showing your passion and that you can be trusted.

▶ *Personal connection.* Nothing's better than a personal connection with a client. If a client likes you, they'll think the best of you.

► *Listening/responding directly to what is required.* The best way to show that you care is by listening carefully and responding appropriately.

► *The work: design impact, tours, demonstrated quality, and so on.* If your work is brilliant (and the client can tell), you'll earn points. If you can demonstrate the value of your work (in how it has saved other clients money, for example), you'll also earn points.

The business development process is about convincing the prospective client that your firm is the best one for the job, within the structure that the client establishes for communications and submissions (qualifications, proposals, presentations, etc.). The process involves identifying targets and opportunities, learning about them, and keeping up with them, getting closer to the client until an architect is selected.

The discussion of the business development process is divided into the following six chapters:

► *Chapter 6—Targets and Opportunities: Finding and Pursuing Leads*

► *Chapter 7—Brochures and Qualifications Packages: Who Are You? What Have You Done?*

► *Chapter 8—Proposals: Making an Offer*

► *Chapter 9—Presentations: The Chemistry Test*

► *Chapter 10—Design Competitions: High Risk and High Impact*

► *Chapter 11—Closing the Deal: Setting the Fee, Negotiating, and Signing the Contract*

As mentioned in the introduction, Part II of this book documents the business development process, but it's a misconception to think that this information is going to teach you how to use the process to get more work. The purpose of Part II is to explain how the game works and what the rules are, so that you can get into the game. From there, it's up to you to use your talents to increase your business.

Targets and Opportunities
Finding and Pursuing Leads

6

Contrary to popular opinion, marketing architectural services is not about putting proposals together and making presentations. It's not about waiting for RFPs to arrive or for public solicitations to be posted in the newspaper or the *Commerce Business Daily*. Marketing is about figuring out where you want your business to go and laying out a path to get there. It's an active process, not a passive one.

You have a choice. You can be responsive or proactive in your marketing. You can either wait for the phone to ring or you can pick up the phone and make the call yourself. It is, of course, easier to be responsive, to wait for the opportunities to find you. It's much harder to make things happen, to discover a real need that a potential client has and to position your firm to serve that need.

Responsive marketing is not generally an effective strategy. By the time the RFP or solicitation hits the street and you burst into action, you may be too late. It's very difficult to win a project without a relationship, and it's tough to build a relationship once the word's out about the upcoming project. It does happen occasionally: An architecture firm that the prospective client barely knows manages to slip in,

RULE OF THUMB

The first rule of marketing: Never wait! Find opportunity, rather than waiting for it to come to you.

blow everybody away, and walk away with the business. But this is so rare as to be nearly mythical. Clients are people, and people generally hire other people they know, like, and trust.

You need to take control of the process, to identify clients that you would like to work for, and reach out to them, building your relationships with them until they give you a chance to prove yourself.

BRIGHT IDEA

Identify clients you would like to work with and reach out to them.

Targeting: Whom Do You Want to Work for?

Start by identifying prospective clients with whom you'd like to do business. Survey the markets that you're currently working in (defined by industry, facility type, service, or geography). Are there clients that you haven't worked for in your markets that you'd like to work for? Make a list of 10 to 20 prospective clients to target.

BRIGHT IDEA

Make a list of possible clients in your target markets.

Be realistic. You need to believe that each potential client on your list is an achievable target for you and your firm. Don't put down organizations for which there are serious roadblocks, such as those that you know only work with firms that are very different from yours (large firms, high-profile design firms, specialists), or organizations for whose projects you have no relevant experience.

Once you've assembled a list of ideal clients, begin to research every potential client on the list. Go online and find out everything you can about them. Ask people you know about them. (See Chapter 12, "Research," for a discussion of how to conduct research on a prospective client.)

Most important, try to connect yourself to the key decision makers in the client organizations. Who are they? What are their backgrounds? Who do you know who knows them? How can you meet them? What can be your pretext for approaching them and getting to know them?

Your Network: Building Relationships

Networking is vital to the success of your business. In a service business (especially a business-to-business service like architecture), a good network can make the difference between a flourishing practice and one that is struggling to survive. Networking is a continual and ongoing process—it doesn't just happen when you have a lead that you're trying to find out more about; it should be ongoing.

BRIGHT IDEA
Use your network to gain information on prospective clients.

TIP

You build you
network by making
new friends.

REMINDER

Include an allowance
for industry events in
your marketing
budget.

Everybody has a network. When you're a child, your network is your immediate family. When you go to school, everyone in your class is in your network. Today, everyone that you know socially or work with (within your firm, consultants, contractors, clients) is part of your network.

Many people think of a network as a set of artificial relationships, a social convention that exists to fulfill a business purpose: sharing and trading information. But your network is essentially a circle of friends. The relationships in your network are real; they are based on authentic interpersonal connections. In networking as in life, be yourself. Don't try to build your network with people you don't like or don't want to be around. You will connect much more easily and naturally with people that you like than with people that you don't—so seek out people that you like.

You build your network the same way that you look for new friends. In social situations—industry events, parties, even on your projects—look for people with whom you feel a natural connection, people to whom you believe you have something to offer, and who have something to offer you. What each side offers the other can be almost anything: industry information, connections, a good laugh, knowledge of the local community, gossip. All that's important is that you like each other and that each has something to offer the other.

If you observe your friends and colleagues, you'll see that people build their networks in different ways. Some people seem as if they want to know everybody; others try to build very tight bonds with a limited number of people; still others try to seek out people who can help them directly. Is there a right way to build your network? Is there some kind of optimal network size you should be striving for? What makes a good network, anyway?

> *Network size:* the number of people in your network

> *Strength of relationships*: how close you are to the people in your network

> *Resources*: access to information, connections; what your network offers you

There isn't a right or wrong way to build a network; you could build a great network with five friends (if the relationships were strong and they had information and connections) or with 600. Your style and focus depends on who you are as a person and what you're trying to achieve. Build as big a network as you're comfortable with.

You need to build and evolve your network constantly. This means, of course, that you must attend industry events and gatherings and that you need to talk to people you don't know. Some people are naturals at this, most of us aren't; but everybody can improve their skills at meeting and talking with new people. All it takes is practice. It's not "schmoozing."

Quality over Quantity

There is some anecdotal evidence that when building a network you should strive for quality over quantity. Some time ago, while talking to a successful businessman and expert networker, he said something surprising: "My career was built with three relationships." Due to his success and his mastery of social skills, I had assumed that there had been thousands of relationships that had helped him get to the top. In fact, he had built thousands of relationships, but those came later. Without three critical friendships, it wouldn't have happened, or it would have been much harder for him.

TIP

Everybody can improve their social skills. All it takes is practice.

TIP

Seek out people you are genuinely interested in, not just business opportunities.

Schmoozing is trying to gain personal advantage by meeting somebody in a social setting. Just because people are often inauthentic in social situations doesn't mean you need to be. Be authentic, seek out people for whom you might have a natural affinity, and try to build a relationship with them.

When you meet someone new, the most important thing to do is to take an active, genuine interest in that person. Ask questions. Listen carefully. If you aren't authentic, if you're just going through the motions or aren't really interested or listening, the person you're talking to will know. (For more on this point, check out Dale Carnegie's classic book, *How to Win Friends and Influence People.*)

It's also important to be enthusiastic. When you're meeting new people, your enthusiasm speaks volumes and can make it much easier for you to make conversation and get your point across. People take interest, pay attention, and respond when they see that you're truly excited about something. If you're genuinely enthusiastic about your profession and the work that you do, people you meet will be interested in hearing more about your firm and your work. You'll have a natural segue to talk about your business and to find out if the person you're talking to works with or hires architects.

In all cases, behave like the professional you are, and seek out others with similar professional values. If you demonstrate a high standard of trustworthiness, people will be drawn to you and will want to help you. They will know that if they help you, you'll remember the favor and return it when they need it. People want to help others that they like and trust. Generally, the only time that people will go out of their way for somebody they don't like, trust, or know is when there's some immediate reciprocal benefit to them. People go out on a limb for their friends, but usually not for their acquaintances.

Networking is always a two-way street. The relationships you have in your network exist for mutual benefit, and you have to help each other in order for your relationships to survive and grow. Ideally, if you've built a strong network of people in related disciplines (engineers, contractors, real estate brokers, developers, consultants), you can share information on upcoming projects (leads). Initially, with newer contacts, your sharing may be more guarded and exploratory: "Have you heard anything about this new project?" With more established contacts, you'll be thinking of projects for each other: "I heard about a new project that would be perfect for your firm."

Use and maintain your network. Call your friends on the phone, go to lunch, have drinks after work—whatever works for you and whatever activities reflect the common interests that you share. Find a comfortable frequency of rotation with the people in your network. How often do you see them? How often do you talk on the phone? How often do you email?

Bear in mind that relationships between people naturally wax and wane. It seems to happen naturally when two people drift apart or when two people find they have a common interest. But we are in control of this process to a large extent—we can decide which relationships are important and which are less so. We naturally focus our energy on the more important relationships and see those friends more often. Don't be afraid to prioritize your network. See the more important contacts more often. Don't hold

REMINDER

Networking is a two-way street. Be ready to help the members of your network at any opportunity.

onto the less important contacts. Don't force a relationship to continue that is naturally waning.

Evaluating Leads: Hot or Cold?

BRIGHT IDEA

If you have a lead that you aren't pursuing, consider passing it on to someone else in your network.

A lead on a potential project can come from practically anywhere—a friend, a work associate, a client, a family member, even the newspaper. If people who know you are familiar with the work that you do, they'll think of you when they hear about new projects that fall within your expertise and interest.

When you hear of a new project from any source, consider it carefully, balancing your enthusiasm with a healthy degree of skepticism. No matter what the project, ask yourself or your source the following questions:

> ► *What's the project?* How big? Where is it? What's the budget?

> ► *What's driving the project?* Why is it happening now? What is changing in the client's business that necessitates this project? What objective is the client trying to achieve?

> ► *Is it for you?* Is this project something that you do? Not just something that you can do, but something that you are truly qualified to do, and experienced in doing?

> ► *Who's the competition?* Which other firms will be considered for this project? If the answer is "none," great! If the answer is "an open field of 50 or 100 firms," not so great.

> ► *What are your relationships?* Who do you know who is involved with this project? Who can you meet? How can you connect yourself to the decision makers?

- *What's the timing?* If you're hearing about the project as word hits the street, or as the project is announced, you may be too late—there may already be other firms lined up to do the project. If you're hearing about it early, while the project is being defined, you are in an ideal position to help with the process and position yourself for the work.

- *Can you get there?* Realistically, given the client, your experience, your relationships, the competition, and the timing, what are your chances of winning this project?

- *What should you do next?* If you want to go after this project, what do you do now?

Finding or inferring the answers to these questions puts you in a much better position to evaluate the lead and determine your level of investment. Many people hear about a lead and rush headlong into the pursuit; it's much better to step back for a second, evaluate the lead objectively, and then determine how high a priority this lead is and the proper course of action.

Developing the Lead: Getting Closer, Somehow

It can't be said too strongly: There is no substitute for personal relationships in the process of developing leads. If you know the decision makers, you are in a far better position to convince them of your abilities and win the work. Relationships with other influencers in the process—other consultants, real estate brokers, friends of the client—can be very helpful as well. The people who "surround" the client can recommend you or can position your firm as the right choice to the client. Ideally, you'd like to have a solid relationship with every decision maker and with everyone who's whispering in their ears.

But what if you don't know anybody? What if you hear about a lead from somebody who is not connected with the project, and who can't introduce you or recommend you to the decision makers?

You have to get closer, somehow. You have to build relationships—fast. The name of the game (as popularized by John Guare's play and film) is the "six degrees of separation." Who do you know who knows somebody who knows somebody who knows somebody? Who do you know who can introduce you to somebody connected with the project? Who can that person introduce you to? Using your network, how can you meet the decision makers? If you can't get to the decision makers, how can you get to people who know the decision makers?

The goal here is to meet people—not to talk to them on the phone. You want to build a personal relationship, and that means you have to meet face to face. If you're meeting for the first time, ask the person introducing you to take you and the new contact out to lunch or to breakfast or for a drink—whatever is most comfortable for the three of you. If you can't get a friend of yours to introduce you personally, at least ask him or her to mention you to the contact; then you can make a "warm call" (as opposed to a "cold call") to discuss the project and make an appointment to meet in person.

When you meet somebody for the first time, your professionalism and your enthusiasm are critical. Take an active interest in the person you are meeting—see him or her as a person, as a valuable contact in his or her own right, not merely as a means to an end. Don't "sell" the person; be an enthusiastic representative of your profession and your firm. Build a relationship, and, hopefully, a friendship.

Cold Calls: Sometimes You Just Have to Pick Up the Phone

No matter how hard you try, there are times when you can't find a connection to the decision makers or to anyone who knows them—your network just isn't able to get you there. In most cases, the fact that you don't have a personal connection will make it very difficult for you to get the project. Not impossible, mind you, just very difficult. If you don't have a connection, it's highly likely that one of your competitors does and that you're beginning the process at a real disadvantage.

Your last recourse is a cold call. It's called a cold call because the person you're calling has no idea who you are. Any warmth that arises from the situation will be your own. Even a warm call would have been better—when the person you're calling has heard about you before. But that possibility has been exhausted. Now your alternatives are reduced to two: Pick up the phone and call "cold," or forget about the lead.

If you're honestly interested in the project and believe that you're qualified, it's still worth a shot. Here are a few basic rules for cold calls:

> ➤ *Know whom you are calling.* Know as many details as you can about the person you want to talk to. Know his or her name, title, role in the project, history, and anything else you can find out before you pick up the phone. The goal of the call is to get a personal meeting. Personal rela-

tionships aren't built over the phone. Have a strong hook (something in your portfolio that the person you're calling will want to see) that will get you the meeting.

➤ *Rehearse what you are going to say.* When you get on the phone with the person, you may not have very much time to break through his or her "sales filter" and convince him or her that it would be valuable to meet you. Plan it, write it down, and rehearse it.

➤ *Be specific.* You're calling to talk about a specific project. Ask about it. Don't be shy about why you're on the phone.

➤ *Ask questions.* Prepare good questions to ask about the project, to show that you've thought about it—not just about the selection process, but about the project itself. Ask questions that the person you're talking to may not have considered.

➤ *Be charming, funny, human—in keeping with your own personality.* Your goal is to build a relationship. Be yourself, have energy, and be as charming and personable as you can.

➤ *Send information, and always follow up.* As a follow-up to your call, always send some information about you and your firm. Make it as specific to the project as possible. It can't just be marketing fluff; it has to be information that will be interesting to the contact.

Again, bear in mind that cold calling is not a particularly effective means to bring in work. It should be your absolute last resort, after you've exhausted your network but still want the project and believe that it's right for you. Relationships, more than any other factor, are what win work, and trying to build a relationship from a cold call is nearly impossible. Think about it: How many friendships have you formed with people who initially called you out of the blue?

Tracking Leads: Finding a System That Works

An important part of the process of pursuing leads is having a system for tracking leads, so that you know what the most recent activity was and what the next steps are. If you're working alone to track a few leads, this system can be fairly simple—using a notebook or a simple spreadsheet. But if you're working with others within your organization, you need to share this information, so you may want to invest in a more robust database system for tracking leads.

Each of us naturally develops a unique system for managing our stuff. A system for managing personal information, such as leads information, call follow-up, and so on tends to be very personal and idiosyncratic in nature. But as the number of people who need to share this information grows, it's important to create a system that everyone can use to view and share information on leads.

Within your organization, there's usually no point in keeping leads information close to the breast. Unless you're pursuing some top-secret lead, there's generally far more to be gained by sharing this information: Others can see what you're doing, can help if they know someone related to the project, and can learn from your example how to pursue leads.

There is no one-size-fits-all system for tracking leads in our industry. You have to find a system that

RULE OF THUMB
Find an effective way to share your leads within your firm.

will work for your organization. See Chapter 13, "Knowledge Management," for a more in-depth discussion of lead-tracking systems and other databases that are useful for marketing.

Brochures and Qualifications Packages

7

Who Are You? What Have You Done?

You have just met a potential client or other new contact, and you want to give them a document that describes who your firm is and the work that you've done. You need a brochure!

Brochures and qualifications are basic introductory documents that provide general information on your firm and your work. The word "brochure" is generally used to refer to a professionally printed and bound document that provides a broad overview of the firm, while the word "qualifications" (typically shortened to "quals") is used to describe customizable documents that are printed in-house and are more exacting in nature, presenting the firm's experience in a specific market or for a specific project.

Using Brochures and Qualifications Documents: Handing Them Over or Sending Them Out

There are number of situations in which a brochure or qualifications document is particularly useful:

- ► Given personally when you meet a new contact in person

- Sent as a follow-up to a personal meeting or phone call
- Given to a friend to pass along to a contact who does not know you
- Sent in response to a request for information on your firm (an RFQ, RFI, or a phone call)
- When your brochure is brand new, sent to your existing clients and contacts as a "refresher"

It isn't usually productive to send a brochure or qualifications package out cold, without having met or spoken to the person you're trying to reach (or utilizing an intermediary who knows you both). A brochure does not take the place of a personal introduction or phone call. If your brochure arrives unsolicited, it will probably be perceived as junk mail, and treated as such. The best way to reach a decision maker is through a personal contact—not by cluttering their inbox with your brochure.

Bring a brochure or a qualifications package when you meet a new contact, or send it along as a follow-up after a meeting or telephone conversation. If you've spoken with the contact about a specific project or a specific type of project, send a qualifications package that highlights your experience in that area. If you've just met, haven't talked specifically about a type of project, and just want to provide a little information, send a general firm brochure, which will broadly cover the full range of work that your firm does.

When you give your brochure or qualifications package to a new contact, it's best to show them what's inside, rather than just handing it over as something for them to look through later. You want to show your contact what's important about your firm, make it clear what's relevant to them, and convey how passionate you are about your work. Your attitude toward the piece will influence theirs, and the personal act of showing them the brochure or qualifications package will make them remember you and what's in the brochure.

Types of Systems: What Are the Options?

Firms use a variety of different kinds of brochure/ qualifications systems to present themselves to prospective clients and other contacts. There are many different options, so you'll need to identify the system that works for your firm and your markets. The system that you select will depend on how "polished" you want your firm to look, how customizable you need your documents to be, and how much money you are prepared to spend. Here are few popular options for brochure/qualifications systems:

> ▶ *Preprinted brochure and customizable qualifications book.* Some firms have a printed brochure on the shelf, as well as a system for assembling customized qualifications. The brochure is generally professionally printed in a quantity of several thousand (in order to make the printing cost-effective). The qualifications materials are usually printed in-house on a Fiery, inkjet, or color laser printer; but for enhanced quality, component pages can also be professionally printed.

> ▶ *Pocket folder with insert pages.* Many firms use a folder system in which to wrap their brochure/ qualifications documents. The folder can have a standard firm brochure bound into it, or the

TIP

When you give your brochure to a prospective client, show them what's inside.

REMINDER

Consider your marketing budget from the beginning. Brochure/qualifications systems can be expensive. Choose a system that achieves your objectives and that you can afford.

firm brochure can slip inside the folder with project pages, reprints, white papers, and other materials. These pieces (except for the folder) can either be printed in-house or be professionally printed.

> *Bind-on-demand brochure/qualifications documents.* Other firms just bind documents together on a totally customizable, as-needed basis. The sheets in the system can be printed in-house or professionally, and are bound in-house to provide a finished look.

BRIGHT IDEA

Collect brochures from other firms—competitors and collaborators—to get an understanding of the context and ideas for your brochure/qualifications package.

Looking at Your Book: Evaluating Your System

Let's say you want to create a new brochure or qualifications book or update your existing system. Begin the process by evaluating your materials to understand where you're starting from, and to provide a basis for comparison. While you may be starting from zero if you're a start-up firm, every firm that has been around for any time at all probably has some documents that they use to describe the firm and their work.

Look at your system—your brochure and qualifications book—with a critical eye. What isn't clear? What would you like to improve or update? What about the system doesn't "feel" like your firm? Apply some basic criteria to your materials. What makes a good brochure or qualifications package?

> *Relevance to the audience:* Does it speak to the reader?

> *Recognizability:* Does it "look like" your firm?

> *Consistency:* Does it fit with the rest of your materials? It is internally consistent?

- *Quality of graphic design:* Does it look good? Is it laid out well?

- *Quality of images:* Are the images striking? Do they reinforce your messages?

- *Quality of writing:* Is it written well?

Ask a client or contact with whom you have a close relationship to comment on your brochure or qualifications package. Choose someone that you know is going to be completely honest with you, and make sure that he or she feels comfortable commenting frankly. Ask: How does our brochure or qualifications book compare to others you've seen? What should we focus on improving? What do you like or dislike about our materials?

 TIP

Compare your brochure to your vision statement. Do they communicate the same ideas and values?

Once you have a clear impression of what works and what doesn't work with your existing materials, you'll be in a much better position to create new materials that improve on your existing ones, and represent your firm in an honest but flattering way.

Document Strategy: Asking the Big Questions

When you start to think about your new brochure or qualifications system, you need to do a little soul-searching and ask yourself three fundamental questions: Who are we? Who are we trying to talk to? What do we want to say? If you've gone through a strategy, branding, positioning, and planning process, as outlined in Chapters 1 to 4, these answers may be easy for you. If you haven't, you'll need to do some thinking now to be clear about the focus and objectives of your brochure or qualifications system.

- *Who are we?* What's our story? What's our image/brand/reputation? What makes us special/unique?

- *Who are we trying to talk to?* Who are we trying to reach? What are their issues/concerns?

- *What do we want to say to them?* What impression do we want to give? What is our message? What is the desired effect of the brochure/qualifications book?

Once you've answered these questions, you'll have a clear picture of the story that you want to tell to your audience. The sharper your focus, the more specific your message, the better your materials will be. It isn't enough to say, "We want our brochure to convey to everyone who picks it up that we're the best architecture firm in this part of the state." You can't be all things to all people, and conveying that you're the best is a tough message to get across. You'll have a much easier time convincing residential developers that you're experts in residential development, for example. Narrow your focus and your message to deepen your impact.

Begin to think about how your message will be conveyed. You'll be using a number of tools: text, images, the design of the overall brochure. Think about what each tool needs to accomplish, and what the overall style of the brochure or qualifications system should be.

Look at other examples of brochures and qualifications packages from your competition or companies in related fields—contractors, consultants, and others. You aren't the first firm to create a firm brochure, and by looking at what else has been created, you can begin to figure out how you'd like your brochure to be perceived relative to the rest. In order to

REMINDER

Defining your audience makes it easier to communicate your message.

create something that stands out, you need to see the pack that you're trying to stand out from.

When you look at the brochures of your competitors and other firms in our industry, you may be surprised to see that all of them look pretty much the same, and even say a lot of the same things ("We're client-focused."). It's a rare brochure that is innovative enough to truly stand out from the crowd. The challenge, then, in creating your brochure is to represent your firm in such a way that you tell your story clearly, and yet seem truly special to your audience.

What's Inside? The Stuff You Put in the Brochure or Book

When you begin to assemble and create materials for your brochure or qualifications book, consider the different types of content that you can use to get your message across. Your mix of content will depend on the type of brochure or qualifications system that you're creating. Generally, a firm brochure provides

BRIGHT IDEA

Look at brochures from other design or service fields. Is there anything you can learn from them?

broad information on the firm, its work, its services, and its key people, while a qualifications system focuses on project experience, but may also include general background information. Here are the main components in a brochure or qualifications book:

1. *Brochure/qualifications book title.* You can call your brochure or book whatever you want. You don't have to use just your firm name or just the name of the market that you're targeting. You can choose a name for effect or that describes what you offer to your target audience.

2. *Firm overview/history.* Think carefully about how you describe your firm. Make your firm sound interesting, and think of a way to recast your story to put your message at the heart of what you do. Whatever you do, don't start with, "Our firm was founded in 1972 in Columbia, Missouri. We are a full-service design firm. Our services include...."

3. *Point-of-view statement.* You have the opportunity in your brochure or qualifications book to say what you really think about the market or the project type. If you're an expert, don't be afraid to show it. What have you learned about this market or project type? What bit of information can you offer to your audience that they may not already know?

4. *Services: list or descriptions?* Make the services that you offer clear to your audience, especially if you offer services that are different from those of your competition in some way.

5. *Project examples/case stories.* You may want to include only your most important projects in your firm brochure and save the rest for your qualifications book. Potentially, your firm

brochure can be used for several years, so you'll want to avoid projects that may seem dated in a year or two.

6. *Key staff biographies.* If you have one or a few staff members who are really experts in a given area, you may want to include their photos and bios.

7. *Client list.* A client list can provide immediate credibility if you've worked for an impressive list of clients.

8. *Office locations.* Don't forget to tell them where you are located, especially if you have offices in more than one place.

9. *Contact information.* Make sure that you provide contact information on your brochure or qualifications book. Your address, your phone number, and your Web address are critical pieces of information.

10. *Pictures:* project images, people images, evocative images. Think carefully about the pictures and images that you would like to include in your brochure or qualifications book. Choose pictures that reinforce your message and demonstrate the quality of your work. Make sure that you have permission to use every image that you plan to include in your brochure from the copyright owner (the photographer, stock photo house, or other source; you're covered if you took the picture or created the image yourself).

As you compile your materials, don't lose sight of the focus of your brochure or qualifications book, the message that you're trying to convey to your audience. It's easy to get on a roll accumulating materials and begin thinking to yourself, "I'll put this in, and this, and this.... What the heck? It's all great stuff! I'll put it all in!" More is not better. You want to include only as much material in your brochure or qualifications package as helps to convey your message to your audience. If you cram in too much information, your point will become less clear, and your reader may miss it.

Building the System: Making the Tools You Need

The process of creating a brochure or qualifications document can be very challenging. It may seem like fun at first, but it can take far longer than you anticipate and can be far more frustrating. There are a number of roadblocks that you should look out for:

▶ *Everybody has an opinion.* Unless you're a one-person firm, or a firm in which only one person's opinion counts, you'll want to ask your colleagues what they think of the new brochure. Be prepared for differences of opinion. Not everybody has the same feelings about the firm and not everybody will like the same pictures. Often the opinions you'll encounter may be quite strong, and it may be very difficult to build a consensus. The danger is that the eventual product will be a lowest-common-denominator solution that everyone can live with, but that nobody loves.

▶ *There's no real deadline.* Creating brochures and qualifications book are often "downtime" tasks, which you'll do between projects or when you have a little time. There usually isn't a hard-and-fast deadline, and you can spend a long time creating the perfect brochure or qualifications

RULE OF THUMB

Focus and clarity are critical. One great picture is better than 10 good pictures; 50 compelling words are much better than 500.

TIP

Make one trusted leader in your firm responsible for directing the creation of the brochure.

Brochures and Qualifications Packages

book—tweaking text, reevaluating images, and soliciting opinions. Just get it done.

- ▶ *You're getting it printed.* If you're having your brochure professionally printed, you're planning on spending a significant amount of money on the brochure and getting a large quantity that you'll want to last for a few years. This isn't a purchase to be taken lightly, so it's easy to obsess over every detail and show your draft to everyone you know. As already noted, at a certain point, you just have decide it's done and send it to the printer. It doesn't have to be perfect. In fact, it can't be.

Generally speaking, the process of creating a brochure or qualifications book is a collaborative effort between somebody who collects and prepares the content (a writer) and a graphic designer who develops the look and feel of the document. Ideally, these two people have a good working relationship and share a similar vision for the brochure or qualifications book. Documents like this can go through many revisions, so it helps if the writer and the designer are also patient with each other.

An important first step in the process of working together on a brochure or qualifications book is to determine the document format:

- ▶ *Paper size.* You can make a brochure any size you want, as long as you're willing to pay to have a standard-sized paper printed and then cropped (if you're printing professionally) or to have someone cut your pages by hand (if you're printing in-house). There's no shame in using 8½ by 11–inch paper (or A4 in Europe). People are used to it, and it fits well in your bag or a folder.

TIP

At a certain point, imperfect though it is, you have to declare it finished. As the saying goes, "Perfect is the enemy of done."

- *Color (four-color, two-color, or halftone).* While mostly everything is full-color these days, you may want to decide on a limited palette for a portion of your brochure, giving the book a touch of elegance and potentially saving you a little money, too.

- *Number of pages.* If you're printing and binding everything in-house, you can make it anything you want. But if you're creating a four-color book to be professionally printed, you can't make a five-page book; it'll probably need to be 4, 8, 16, or 32 pages.

- *Printing (professionally or in-house).* It's important to decide which components of your system will be printed professionally and which will be printed in-house. The difference in quality will be apparent, so it won't really work to combine materials that are professionally printed and printed in-house in the same book. If you're having materials printed professionally, check with a printer to understand the cost implications of your decisions before you begin design. A printer should be able to give you a reliable quote for your job with just a few specifications: paper size, color, number of pages, binding method, quantity.

Once you've decided on a format and have your production team in place, all you have to do is create the brochure or book. Be prepared to go through a hundred revisions and to entertain thousands of opinions from your colleagues, your staff, and everybody else you know. Try not to lose sight of your message and your audience, and try to stay true to your decisions on format and content. Set deadlines for yourself, and keep them. Creating a brochure or qualifications book can take a year, or it can take a month. Try to complete your book as quickly as you can, but don't settle for something you're not happy with.

When you're in the middle of working on the brochure or qualifications book, try to look at it from a distance, to see it through the eyes of its intended audience. Put your draft down on the floor, stand over it, and say to yourself, "Do I like this brochure? Do I like this firm? Do I want to hire this firm to work for me? Does this look like an exciting firm?" Be honest with yourself, and be prepared for the answers. If you're not satisfied, if the brochure or book doesn't meet the requirements of the potential client in your head, change it. Better to try to improve it now than to realize you don't like it after it's printed.

Proposals
Making an Offer

8

Proposals are important, but not as important as you might think. If you were to analyze the actual marketing expenditures of architectural firms, you'd probably find that most firms spend a disproportionate amount of money—in terms of both hard and soft costs—on proposals. Many firms behave as if the proposal is the main event, that the project is either won or lost at the proposal stage, and so spend a lot of effort creating proposals. They "dress to impress" with custom covers; full-bleed, full-color spreads; and custom layouts that make the proposal look like a magazine.

Despite the amount of effort firms expend on their proposals, it's exceptionally rare that an architectural firm will be selected on the basis of its proposal alone. As discussed earlier in this book, clients tend to hire people they like and trust, people they want to work with. The proposal can help you to convince a prospective client that you're the right choice, but no matter how good your proposal is, no client is going to hire you just because you submitted a great proposal. You have to meet. When you meet the client—whether it's an informal meeting or in a presentation or interview setting—that's your real opportunity to convince them that you're the right firm for the job.

So, if the proposal doesn't get you hired, how does it fit into the business development process? What's it supposed to do? In a conventional selection process, proposals enable the client to make a short list of firms that will then be invited to give a presentation. Marketing common sense dictates that the purpose of the proposal is simply to get you short-listed, to get you to an interview. But that isn't quite right either. Your proposal has to get you to an interview; but when you walk into the interview, you already want to be in first place in the client's mind. While it won't win you the job, the proposal can get you pretty close, and then you can finish the job at the interview.

Sometimes, you may actually have the opportunity to meet the client and present your qualifications before the proposal is submitted. There may not be a second interview, depending on the client and the competition for the project. In this case, your proposal has to validate the choice that is in the client's mind after meeting you. If the client likes you, your proposal must justify their selection—in terms of approach, qualifications, and fee.

So a proposal isn't the end-all-be-all of the marketing process, but it is a critical piece of communication between you and your prospective client. The proposal doesn't win the job; it defines the job. The proposal describes the services that you intend to perform, the anticipated time frame, and the compensation that you expect to receive. Often, the proposal also includes your qualifications to perform the services you're proposing, including your experience and the resumés of the members of your project team. If the client approves your definition of the project (services, schedule, and fee) and believes that you are qualified to perform the proposed services, you will likely make it to the next step in the selection process, which may be an interview or (if you've already met) an opportunity to negotiate. The role of the proposal is to position you to win the project by presenting a clear, unified case for why you are the client's best choice for the project.

Architectural proposals are generally requested and prepared only once a project is "real"; that is, once the potential client has decided that they are going to proceed with the project. Proposals are prepared in response to a request from the prospective client or the client's representative (broker, developer, owner's representative, project/program manager, construction manager, etc.). Sometimes the request is conveyed verbally ("Give me a proposal for this job"), and other times the request is conveyed in writing, in the form of a request for proposal (RFP). In any case, by the time this request is issued, the client has considered the project carefully and defined it in their head to some extent. All the details may not be worked out, but there is probably some kind of vision, some set of objectives that the project is intended to accomplish, and some established parameters in terms of schedule and budget for the project. When you propose, it's important to know as much as you can about the project as defined in the client's head, so that your proposal accurately responds to the client's vision.

The Go/No-Go Decision: Is It Worth It or Not?

Okay, don't get too excited. Calm down; take a deep breath. So you've got an RFP, or you heard about a

REMINDER

Once an RFP is put out, you will have much more competition to get the client's attention. Ideally, you want to have a relationship with the client well before the RFP is issued.

TIP

Your research shows your enthusiasm for the project. Before you submit your proposal, it's important to find out as much as you can about the client and the project.

new project from a government leads source. Before you begin writing that project approach or editing your resumé, you need to decide if the project is worth going after.

If you're like many professionals, your immediate reaction may be, "Worth going after? Of course it's worth going after! We need the work!" You may very well need the work, but that doesn't mean that the RFP in your hand is the answer to all of your troubles, or that it makes sense to spend time and money chasing this particular opportunity.

Not all projects are gems. Not all projects make money. Not all projects help to build your portfolio. Some projects are painful experiences that can hurt you in the long run. And that's *if* you can win them. If you have no chance of winning, what's the point of submitting?

TIP

Sometimes you just have to say no to an opportunity.

Some firms have complex "go/no-go" forms that they fill out for every opportunity, in order to decide if a project is worth pursuing or not. They answer a list of questions with values from 1 to 5 or 1 to 10 and then come up with an apparently objective score that tells them whether they should pursue this opportunity. I'm not a fan of the scorecard method of deciding whether to go after a project, but you do need some method, and if a quantitative system works for you, go ahead and create a scorecard. I prefer working with five simple questions. If you're truly going to pursue a project, your answers to these questions should be yes: Do we want it? Can we win it? If we win it, can we do it? Can we make money doing it? And, will it help the firm?

> *Do we want it?* Why are you interested? Will this project build your portfolio? Is it an exciting design opportunity? Is it a project that gives you

a chance to do what you do best? Is it just a bread-and-butter moneymaker? How does this project fire your passion? It's much harder to win a project you don't care about than one you're passionate about.

- *Can we win it?* Can you present a compelling case for why yours is the right firm for this project? Can you beat the competition? Will the client consider you a credible choice to do this project? Do you already have a relationship with the client? If you don't have a shot, you're better off devoting your energies to other opportunities.

- *If we win it, can we do it?* The last thing you want is to win a project and then not be able to deliver, either because you don't have the workforce or you don't have the expertise. Failing on your commitments can cause a lot of harm to your reputation and to your relationships. Only go after a project when you know that you can deliver on your promises.

- *Can we make money doing it?* You don't need to make money on every project, but you certainly need to make money on most. You can't operate at a loss (and no one expects you to). Don't take a project you can't make a profit on, unless it's a calculated risk to enable you to enter a new market or to increase your firm's profile. Make a smart business decision at the proposal stage, and be very cautious about projects that don't seem as if they'll be profitable.

- *Will it help the firm?* There are lots of ways that the right project can help you—building your portfolio, making new relationships, getting press, improving the impression of your firm in the minds of people in the industry and the general public. You want to pursue projects that can help you in one way or another.

Though it's best if every project you go after merits a yes answer to all of these questions, there are, of course, exceptions. Occasionally a project will appear that you will want desperately for one reason or another, to such an extent that it outweighs all other concerns. Sometimes you need to take risks. For example, if it's a project that you've always wanted to do, but you know that you don't have a chance at winning it, you may still want to submit, against the odds. Follow your heart, but ask yourself these five questions. Make sure that most of the projects you pursue are projects that you want, that you can win, that you can do, that will make you money, and that will ultimately help you in one way or another.

There are also times when you do need to submit just to let a particular client (either public or private sector) know that you're out there and that you're interested in working for them. Don't, however, do this any more often than you absolutely have to. If you receive an RFP for a project that you know you can't win or that just isn't for you, consider sending a letter that says, "Thank you for this opportunity, but this project isn't for us, and we believe you'll be much better served by another firm. Please keep us in mind for other projects." You don't necessarily need to send a proposal to show that you're interested.

Once you've decided that you are going after a project, the next important decision is how much effort you're going to put into the proposal and presentation. In other words, it's definitely a "go," but is it just a "go" or is it a "go go go!" This will probably

TIP

If you don't want the project or don't think that you can win, don't submit a proposal. Send a letter instead.

depend as much on you as on the opportunity: How much do you want the project? How much time do you have to spend? How hard of a fight do you think it will be to win? If it's a "go go go" project, one that you're really committed to winning, be prepared to pull out all the stops.

Proposal Strategy: Making It Clear That You're the Right Choice

A proposal should never just be a perfunctory response to an RFP. Ideally, your proposal is the embodiment of your strategy for convincing the prospective client that yours is the right firm to do the job. It should be a cohesive statement to the client that says, "We want this job and we're the right firm to do it."

In order to formulate a strategy for the proposal, you need to consider carefully the client and their goals and vision for the project. Whether the proposal was requested verbally or in writing, listen attentively to everything the client says. Try to find the answers to basic questions about the project that give a context to the overall project and to the selection process:

- ► Who is the client?
- ► What is the project?
- ► What is the client trying to accomplish?
- ► What are the parameters of the project (scope, schedule, budget, etc.)?
- ► What is the history of this project? Why now?
- ► Which other architects are being considered?
- ► Who will make the decision about which architect to select?

> What's the selection process?

> What's the criteria for selection?

If it's not clear from the RFP, ask. Asking the client questions makes it clear that you're listening, you're thinking, and you're interested in the project. Ask in person, over the phone, or via email—by whatever means is preferred by the client.

Conduct research to fill in the gaps. Who is this client? What is their business or primary activity? Have they been mentioned in the news? Go online and check out their Web site and third-party sources. Ask people you know about the client and/or the project. Try to find out everything you can. (See Chapter 12 for a discussion of research process and techniques.)

As you're thinking about the project, try to imagine why you and your firm might be the client's best choice for this project. Do you have significant relevant experience? Do you have special expertise that other firms may not have? Is there some special resource that you bring to the project that no other firm has?

State your strategy as clearly and simply as you can. "We're the right choice for this laboratory building because we've designed 12 buildings like this in the last five years. Labs like this are what we do best and what we love to do." Once you've formulated your strategy, prepare your entire proposal to reinforce your strategy.

Setting a Price: What Should We Charge?

At its core, a proposal is a description of services and a fee to perform the services described. Everything

BRIGHT IDEA

The Internet is a great way to find out the buzz about the prospective client.

TIP

The more you know about your audience, the better prepared you will be to persuade them.

else is secondary, and serves to support and justify your proposed services and compensation.

It can sometimes seem that clients hire architects based exclusively on fee. Most of the time, this isn't the case; the fee is only one factor evaluated among many. Most clients look for value, rather than simply the lowest fee. When you submit a proposal, your fee is considered in context with your competitor's fees. If it seems out of alignment with the competition (either too low or too high, given your proposed services, perceived quality, and desirability), you will likely not be selected for the project. If your fee is too high, you may be perceived as not a good value; if your fee is too low, you may be perceived as naive about the effort the project requires (or, sometimes, as a really great deal).

Generally, fee is not the deciding factor, but a *justifying* factor. Fee is used to explain a choice rather than make one. If a client wants to hire you, the client will find a way to make the fee work, if possible. However, if a client doesn't want to hire you, it's very easy to say, "Your fee was too high" and to select another firm.

Assigning a fee to provide services for a project is a complicated process. As consumers, we generally perceive cost as a direct result of quality. We assume that if a television or a car or a computer costs more, it must in some way be better than one that costs less. The same is true of architectural services. You will, to some extent, be perceived as providing a commensurate service for your fee. If you're expensive, you'll be perceived as providing more or better service than if you're cheap. There are many strategies to try to navigate the expected perceptions of your targets: charging higher rates but being "worth it," optimizing delivery to charge the lowest prices in town, aiming for the middle to be a "good value," and so on.

Once you have some idea how much you will charge for the services you're proposing, the next challenge is deciding how to express your fee, and what conditions to base it on. The following are a few common ways to represent architectural fees:

- ▶ *Lump sum, based on area (dollar per square foot).* Fees are expressed as a dollar value based on a cost-per-square-foot number. If the size of the project changes, it is easy to renegotiate fees.

- ▶ *Lump sum, based on construction cost (percentage of total construction cost).* Fees are expressed as a dollar value based on a percentage of the total construction budget. If the project budget changes, fees can be renegotiated.

- ▶ *Time and materials (based on hourly rates).* Hourly rates for each member of the team are given. These rates include all direct and indirect personnel costs—including benefits, overhead, real estate, and so on. The client is billed for staff time at these rates, as well as expenses.

▶ *Not-to-exceed (based on area and hourly rates).* This is a hybrid of the time and materials method and the lump sum method. Fees are calculated based on hours billed to the project at given hourly rates, up to a not-to-exceed maximum (sometimes called a *maximum upset fee*) usually based on project area.

However you represent your fee, make sure that you provide enough conditions to protect yourself. Exclude any services that you are not prepared to include, but may possibly be construed as part of your basic services and fee. State clearly any parameters upon which your fee is conditioned, such as schedule, project terms, contract terms, and so on.

Proposal Organization: Choosing a Structure That Serves You

RULE OF THUMB

In determining your fee, be specific about the services that you include or exclude from your proposal.

Organize your proposal in a way that supports your strategy. Clearly, if the RFP specifies a preferred order for the submission to follow, you shouldn't deviate from it without a good reason. But if the RFP doesn't specify a table of contents, create your own that serves your strategy. Be clear and logical, and try to use the proposal to tell the story of why the client should select you. Here's a sample organization:

1. *Cover letter.* A cover letter, coming at the very front of the proposal and addressed directly to the client, will probably be read more closely than the rest of the document. It's a great opportunity to state clearly and simply why you are the right choice for the project. Be specific, and avoid clichés like, "We are uniquely qualified."

2. *Project understanding.* You have to define the problem before you can solve it. It's always a good idea to repeat back what you've heard about the project to the client. This confirms that you've been listening and that you understand the client's goals. It also enables you to define the project in a way that positions you as the right firm for this project.

3. *Project approach.* Okay, so what are you going to do? Not in terms of a step-by-step methodology (that can come in the next section), but in terms of an overall vision for the project. How are you going to respond to the client's challenges? What are you going to offer? What resources or special processes do you propose to utilize?

4. *Scope of services.* Now you can describe your step-by-step process. Make it clear and as concise as you can, but include enough detail to protect yourself against any misinterpretation. This is what you propose to do for the fee that you are expressing in your proposal. Make it unambiguous, and provide specific numbers (number of revisions, document sets, presentations, etc.) where there could be any possible confusion.

5. *Project schedule.* How long is the project going to take to design and build? Are there any special innovations that you can offer to complete the project faster (if this is an important priority) or to better utilize the time that you have?

6. *Proposed team.* Who's going to do the work? Be clear about who the people are, what each is going to do (saying "project manager" isn't enough for a client that isn't familiar with the design process), and what their individual qualifications are.

7. *Relevant experience.* What have you done before that is similar and relevant? You may be able to use standard "project pages" from your qualifications book (see Chapter 7) if you've developed them. But you may need to customize the descriptions of your projects to be more relevant to the project you're pursuing. In any case, don't include too many projects. Three projects that are exactly the same as the project you're pursuing are plenty. You may need more if your experience is indirectly relevant.

8. *Compensation.* State your compensation simply and clearly. Provide information on consultants, reimbursables, additional services, taxes, and anything else that may affect the cost to the client for professional services to complete this project. Include enough detail (assumed area, schedule, etc.) to protect yourself in case the project changes.

Keep in mind that the preceding is a *possible* basic organization for your proposal. There is no standard proposal; each should be highly customized to respond to the specific priorities of the prospective client and the specific requirements of the project. If you're responding to an RFP, expect to be required to provide lots of other information, including your firm's finances, your insurance, your quality assurance processes, your project management and/or design philosophy, your current workload, and more. Always respond fully to any questions asked by the RFP, in the order that they are asked.

Government proposals and qualifications generally require that you respond on a standard form. Some institutional and large private-sector clients also have a proposal or qualifications form. The forms vary by agency, organization, and level of government, but many of the forms are currently based on the Federal Government's Standard Forms 254 and 255. (At the time of this writing, the federal government is changing to a new standard qualifications form, the SF 330, and it isn't clear if or when state and local governments, colleges and universities, and other organizations will change their forms as well.) Familiarize yourself with the forms that are used by the organization or agency to which you're proposing, and fill them not just completely and accurately, but, ideally, as the agency expects you to fill them out. This can take experience to figure out, but it's important: government submissions are generally evaluated against a checklist, and if you don't meet the organization or agency's minimum criteria, your submission will probably end up in the "no thanks" pile.

Proposal Values: What Makes a Proposal Good?

In preparing your proposal, it helps to have certain aspirations for the quality of your submission, a set of "values." Accepting a set of values for your proposals enables you to evaluate your submissions in accordance with your standards and to pinpoint what you can improve next time. Here is a basic set of proposal values. A proposal should be:

> ▶ *Clear.* Your proposal should clearly describe the services that you propose to provide, and should be explicit about the reasons that your firm is the right choice for this project.

> ▶ *Concise.* Nobody has time to read more words than are necessary to express an idea. Your proposal should be as concise as possible, including

only that information that is essential to describe your approach and highlight your qualifications.

- ▶ *Correct.* Proofread your proposal before you submit it. Stupid mistakes are common under tight deadlines, and can reflect poorly on you and your firm. Make sure you spell the client's name correctly, refer to their organization correctly, and calculate your fee correctly.

- ▶ *Responsive.* Respond directly to the client and their concerns, whether the request for proposal was issued verbally or as a written RFP. Don't offer services in your proposal that are not warranted by this project. Answer completely all the questions in the RFP.

- ▶ *Specific.* Be as precise as possible about what you are proposing for this project. Describe your process in detail; specify the number of meetings, number of revisions, number of schemes, and so on.

- ▶ *Personal.* A proposal is created by one person or group of people for another person or group of people. Address your proposal to its audience. Make it as personal as possible.

- ▶ *Cohesive.* The proposal should look and feel like a single unified document. It should appear custom-crafted, not assembled from disparate parts. Take the time to connect all the dots.

- ▶ *Attractive.* Your proposal should reflect the design style of your firm. The proposal should be attractive, without being overdesigned.

Feel free to add your own values, to provide a yardstick by which you can measure the quality of your submissions. One firm might say, "Our proposal must be creative." Another would add, "Our proposals must reflect our firm's brand." Use the eight points given here as a starting point and develop your own criteria from there.

Proposal Tips and Tricks: Do This, But Don't Do That

The topic of proposals deserves its own book, and fortunately it has already been written, by Frank Stasiowski, as part of the Architect's Essentials series. If you need to know more about proposals, check out his book. Stasiowski is one of the founding fathers of professional services marketing, and he has a lot of great ideas about proposals.

FOR MORE INFORMATION

Read *Architect's Essentials of Winning Proposals,* by Frank Stasiowski (John Wiley & Sons, Inc., 2003).

Before we move on, let me give you a few tips and tricks for the proposal strategy and production process:

> *Know your client.* The proposal is like a love letter to a client. You have to know who they are to write to them. Find out as much as you can and tailor every word to their concerns and personality.

> *Never wait.* Every minute counts. If you receive an RFP and the proposal is due in two weeks, use the time. Meet with everybody who's going to work on the proposal, do research, figure out your strategy, and start writing. Don't let an RFP sit on your desk.

> *Build the right team.* Think carefully about other firms you can team with for large or complex projects. Even if you don't have specific experience, you can be selected for a portion of a project, if you build the right team.

> *Customized boilerplate.* Start the proposal with boilerplate text, then customize it extensively to

reflect this client and project. Start writing from a blank page only if boilerplate text doesn't help you—such as in a project understanding or a very personal cover letter.

- *Write first things last.* Writing and assembling the proposal is a process of refining your strategy. Start with the easy stuff—the team, the experience, the firm information—then work your way back to more specialized and customized information, such as the scope, the understanding, the approach. Write the cover letter last, as by then you'll have a full understanding of what you're proposing and why yours is the right firm.

- *Who writes what?* When you receive the RFP, meet with your proposal team and figure out your strategy, then make assignments for who should write/assemble what. A scope and schedule should be written by the project manager or director, as he or she is going to have to own the project process and live with it for the life of the project. Don't let one person (no matter who it is) get stuck with writing/assembling everything. A proposal should be a team effort, just as the project will be.

- *Say something.* When you write, always try to say something. It may sound simple, but many people miss this point. As you write, ask yourself, "What am I saying?" Use the proposal to say something to your client about the project, to provide some fresh perspective or proposed innovation. Don't be afraid to be smart.

- *Watch the legal stuff.* Proposals can be considered legal documents. Don't make promises you can't keep. Be careful about using words like "guaranty" and "warranty" and statements like, "We will complete the project on time." The client can try to hold you to it, even if circumstances beyond your control cause you to slip. Also be aware that you can't refer to someone as an "architect" unless he or she is registered in the state in which you're proposing to provide your services.

➤ *Follow up.* After you submit the proposal, always call to follow up, within a day. Make sure the proposal was received, see if there are any questions, and find out about next steps. Calling to follow up not only can provide you with information, it also shows the client that you are truly interested in the project.

One last tip to close: Have a positive attitude, and try to make it fun. Many people dread writing proposals. They seem to view it as extraneous, an inessential part of the process that is wasteful and arbitrary. To some extent, they may be right. But the client has asked for certain information from you with regard to a certain project. The proposal is an opportunity for you to put your best foot forward, say what you think, and show your stuff. You get to figure out how you're going to do the project and why you're the best choice to do it. Make the most of it. If you enjoy rising to the challenge and creating a great document for the client, your passion will come through in the proposal and you'll be a more attractive choice to the client. Fun is appealing and contagious, so try to have some.

Presentations
The Chemistry Test

9

You've been short-listed and invited to an interview. Your qualifications, your proposal, your reputation, and all your work to build a relationship with the client have gotten you here. Now what? How are you going to convince the client, in person and beyond any doubt, that yours is the right firm for this project?

The presentation is where it really counts—where the client decides whom they want to work with. Your proposal may get you to this point, but now it's sink or swim. If you blow it here, you've probably blown it completely; it's nearly impossible to recover from a bad interview.

Even if you're presenting before the proposal is submitted, the interview is still the critical point in the decision-making process. If the proposal comes later, it will be used to justify the choice that the client makes when interviewing the candidate firms. As the saying goes, you won't have a second chance to make a first impression.

So what is the client going to base their decision on? You. As discussed in the introduction to this book, clients hire people they like and trust. The

REMINDER

You are the most tangible representation of your firm.

presentation is a chemistry test. The client may have a lot of questions in their head (Can you do the job? Is your fee too high? Are you too busy?), but the most important questions are two: "Do I like you?" and "Can I trust you?" If they like you and trust you, all the other questions become less important.

Since it's all about you, it's pointless to drive yourself up a wall focusing on perfecting your materials. You need to put together a presentation that makes you look good. You want your firm to come across as the right one for the project, and you want to make the client like you and trust you.

By the time you're invited to present, you've probably had some time to think about the project. You've most likely spoken with or met the client already. Through the process of writing your proposal, hopefully you've developed an approach to the project and come up with the reasons why your firm is the ideal choice. If so, you're ready to prepare the presentation.

When you begin to work on the presentation, don't just pull out the PowerPoint you used for your last presentation, change the client's name, and think that you're ready to go. You need to create a custom presentation for this client and project. This doesn't necessarily mean you have to build it from scratch; but you do have to think about the presentation from a fresh perspective, starting from what you want to say to this client about this project. Then, once you've figured out what you want to say, you can review your existing materials, select those that will help you make your points, and create new materials to help you make points you haven't made before.

Presentation Strategy: What Do You Want to Tell Them?

As soon as you find out that you've been short-listed, call the client, thank them for the opportunity to present, and ask a few questions. This enables you to show your enthusiasm for the project and to demonstrate that you're on top of things. Here are some questions that you may want to ask:

- ▶ When is the interview?
- ▶ Where is it (usually, the client's office or yours)?
- ▶ To whom will we be presenting? (How many people? What are their positions in the organization?)
- ▶ How long will we have to present?
- ▶ Is there anything in particular that you'd like us to talk about?
- ▶ Were there any questions raised by our proposal that we should clarify in the presentation?
- ▶ Whom should we bring with us to the presentation (entire team, core team only, consultants, etc.)?
- ▶ Do you have any preference in terms of presentation method or style (PowerPoint, boards, informal, etc.)?
- ▶ (If the interview is in the client's office) What is the room like? How big is it? Is it equipped with presentation technology (screen, projector, pin-up wall, flip charts, etc.)?
- ▶ How many firms are short-listed?
- ▶ Who are they?
- ▶ In your opinion, what's going to make the difference here? What's your selection going to be based on? What should we not forget?

Listen very carefully to the answers. You've been short-listed because the client is seriously considering you for this project. Your proposal (and the relationship-building and qualifications that came before it) convinced the client that your firm could be the right choice. It's very likely that the client will now, more than ever, be clear with you about what the situation is, what you should and shouldn't do, what the real issues are. Unless the client has already picked another firm in their mind (in which case this entire process is a formality), you're probably going to be able to get some good information. Listen well and use the knowledge that you gain wisely.

Don't base your presentation on what you want to say, but on what your client wants to hear. Take your lead from the client, and structure your presentation around the points that they mentioned were important. Consider the tone of your presentation carefully. How formal or informal will it be? To some extent, the client sets the tone, but you can certainly influence it by how you structure the presentation, how you behave, and how you prepare.

Usually, the larger the selection committee and the larger the presentation team, the more formal your presentation will be. Some presentations are very formal, with the presenters talking in a carefully scripted manner, without much interruption, to a selection committee. Other presentations are informal, and can sometimes (if you're lucky) slip into a conversation with each side asking questions of the other: What else can you tell us about the project? What else can you tell us about your approach?

One of the advantages of an informal presentation is that you can get feedback and information in real time, while you're presenting. Generally speak-

BRIGHT IDEA

Prepare a response for hard questions before the interview.

Presentations: The Chemistry Test

ing, a presentation is successful if you are able to address issues that respond to the concerns of your audience. In a formal presentation, however, you have to know what the issues are when you enter the room. With an informal presentation, you can learn about the client's issues as you go along and adjust the presentation accordingly. When you talk about your relevant experience, you can present your previous projects in a way that demonstrates that these projects were solutions to similar challenges that this client is facing. When you describe your project approach, you can assure the client that this approach will ensure that you are able to meet the goals for the project that they have just articulated.

Different types of people tend to be successful in formal and informal presentations, because each requires different skills. Formal presentations require showmanship and raw presentation/public speaking skills: You have to stand well, express yourself clearly, and hit all your points. In informal presentations, listening and interpersonal skills are much more critical: How well do you respond to what the client is saying to you? How well do you "click" with the client?

Whether you're planning a formal or informal presentation, create an agenda that includes everything you want to say. Consider the attributes that differentiate your firm for this project, and address each one in the presentation. Plan who will attend the presentation and make sure that each person will have a chance to speak. Here's an example of a basic agenda:

1. *Introduction.* Introducing the team, the firm, and the project.

2. *Project discussion.* Talking about the project: expressing your understanding of the project

BRIGHT IDEA

Practice what you intend to preach. Run through your entire presentation at least once before you are in front of the client.

and getting the client talking to validate your understanding and identify key issues, goals, challenges, concerns, and so on.

3. *Team organization.* Describing the structure of the team that will provide the required services to accomplish the client's objectives.

4. *Relevant experience.* Talking about what you've done before that is similar to this project.

5. *Project approach.* Describing your approach to this project. How are you going to do it? How are you going to respond to the special challenges of this project? Are you offering any unique services or techniques?

6. *Schedule and budget control.* Reviewing your control methods and plan to assure the client that you will be able to complete the project on time and within their budget requirements.

7. *Conclusion.* Summing up; providing a summary as to why yours is the right firm for this project and emphasizing your commitment and enthusiasm.

8. *Q&A.* Answering questions.

Based on how formal or informal your presentation is, you may or may not want to hand out your agenda. Doing so shows that you're in control, that you're serious, and that you're prepared, but it may be too formal for your client or for the tone of the presentation.

This agenda is only a generic sample. Structure yours to hit any issues that may respond to the concerns of your audience. If sustainability is an issue, highlight it in your agenda. If this project is in Billings, Montana, and your firm is from Spokane, Washington, make sure you talk about your experience in Billings, and how you're going to mobilize to do a project 500 miles from home.

Presentation Materials: Which Tools Are You Going to Use?

People obsess over their presentation materials. It's worse than that, actually. Presentation materials often become a fetish, a totem, a crutch. When preparing a presentation, many people (especially architects) throw all their energy into creating the perfect organization chart, the perfect process diagram, and ignore the real heart of the presentation: the presenter, and the message.

Presentation materials exist to help you enhance the clarity of what you're saying. They're secondary. The show is you, not the PowerPoint. You don't need a PowerPoint. You don't need boards. All you need to give a presentation is you, and maybe a piece of paper and a pencil.

When you think about materials for your presentation, consider the medium carefully. Technology has reached a point in the last few years where it is finally possible (and not prohibitively expensive) to produce any format of materials for your presentation that you might like. You want to wrap the building with your org chart? No problem. You want to make a movie that shows you walking the job site? Sure, why not? While the medium may always have been the message, now you can actually choose your medium at will.

Boards or PowerPoint? Books or a flip chart? A movie or a Flash animation? It's the presenter's choice; there is no longer a technical need for a default medium. Pick what works best for you, the audience, and the message you want to get across.

If you're presenting to a 100-person selection committee, you don't have much choice but to prepare a PowerPoint or a slide presentation. If it's three people across a table, you can use a booklet or photos or boards or a napkin. When you're presenting to 10 or 12 people, you're somewhere in the middle: You either need a PowerPoint, large boards, or (worst case) some kind of handout that your audience can flip through.

Here's a brief summary of the major choices open to you for presentation materials:

- ▶ *PowerPoint.* Currently falling from favor, PowerPoint has been the de facto standard in presentations for the last 10 years or so. Its strengths: easy, cheap, quick, looks good. Its weaknesses: linear (hard to jump around), relentless (awkward to turn the thing off and on), lights need to be turned off or dimmed for the projector (nap time!), tough to resist the urge to put every point you're going to make in bullet-list form on your slides.

- ▶ *Slides.* Slides were PowerPoint before we had PowerPoint. Slides have all the weaknesses of PowerPoint with only one advantage: They look fantastic. You can't beat slides for projecting an image that looks incredible. Strength: image quality. Weaknesses: expensive, slow, hard to make, linear, relentless, lights dimmed or off, text slides suffer from bullet-listitis.

- ▶ *Flash.* Many people in the know think Flash is tomorrow's PowerPoint. What's better than a relentless stream of 100 slides? A relentless stream of 100 slides with animation! Don't you believe it. Strength: Appropriately named, Flash sure is flashy. Weaknesses: Time-consuming (and therefore costly), difficult to customize, has to be projected (so lights off or dimmed).

To its credit, a Flash presentation can be designed to be either linear or nonlinear, as either a movie or slideshow, or an interactive presentation.

- *Boards and banners.* The old favorite. What's better than paper? Today, you can print your materials, as big as you want them, on a wide variety of materials—paper, vinyl, even fabric! You can print full-color photographs, you can print diagrams, you can print text. And then you can mount the materials on foamcore or gatorboard or some other material to make them stiff. Strengths: comfortable and natural; normal lighting. Weaknesses: You need to know how big the room is and how big the audience is to know how big your boards should be and how many you can have. They're also expensive to produce and somewhat burdensome to transport.

- *Flip chart.* A flip chart is basically a bunch of boards printed on paper, bound together and presented one after the other, in PowerPoint style. It's sort of a low-tech PowerPoint (the irony is that it takes a lot more technology to print a full-color large-format page than to make a PowerPoint). Flip charts are a good choice when you'd like to use boards, but you've got too many to carry. Strengths: normal lighting; not particularly cumbersome. Weaknesses: linear, expensive to produce.

- *Handouts.* Often a back-up strategy in case the PowerPoint breaks, you can hand out copies of your presentation and talk your audience through it while they turn pages. Strengths: relatively easy to produce, easy to carry, only moderately expensive; natural lighting. Weaknesses: linear, turn-ahead factor (people are going to leaf through the book while you're talking, rather than focusing on you).

▶ *Show and tell.* If you can get away from using your presentation materials as a script or crutch, just bring stuff you want to talk about. Bring the construction documents of the last project you completed. Bring a model or process book from a relevant project. Bring pictures of projects the client might be interested in. Strengths: no risk of reading the words on the screen to the client; truly interactive (as you talk the client through the materials, they can set the pace and ask questions), nonlinear (you can skip around), comfortable; normal lighting. Weakness: Can be aimless and scary, especially for a less experienced presenter.

In selecting materials, there is a tremendous difference between those that are linear in nature (PowerPoint, slides, flip charts, handouts) and those that are nonlinear (boards, show and tell). Linear materials require that you have your entire presentation planned out precisely, before you walk into the room, and that you execute it as planned. Once you start talking, all you can really do to adapt the presentation to new information is awkwardly skip over a topic; you can't skip around easily. With nonlinear materials, you can rearrange items as you go if the presentation calls for it. You can follow the client's direction, talk about something that the client is interested in for a while, and then skip back to your summary for the close. With nonlinear materials, you can plan everything perfectly and still have the flexibility to rearrange your presentation on the fly, in real time.

The "presentation as crutch" problem cannot be overstated. Many presenters use their materials as their notes for the presentation. They flash up a text-heavy PowerPoint, and then follow the PowerPoint's lead like a presenting machine, taking the audience through every bullet point on every slide. What audience actually enjoys being lectured to in this way, or gets much out of it? Boredom is the natural consequence of this kind of presentation. Keep your notes to yourself. Make sure that the text that you show is there for your audience's benefit, not for yours. Show the audience only the text that you *really* want them to remember. If you show an audience too much text, they aren't going to read it, let alone remember it. If your point is just as effective spoken as displayed on the screen, then speak it—don't write it.

Your materials should strive to show, rather than tell, something to your audience. Don't just put a list of points up there and expect them to be remembered. Find a way to make every point visual. For every reason that you believe the client should select you, show something visual that underscores the reason. Find ways to demonstrate what makes you special, rather than just talking about it.

One way to demonstrate how good you are is to find a place to bring the process of architecture into the presentation—not by showing some kind of process diagram, but by drawing. Find a way to get the client talking, and work with them to work something out on paper —how their façade will look, how to plan their new office—while you're there in a presentation. Show the client what makes you special right there, in real time. Architecture is powerful stuff. The client is looking for an architect to do things that they can't do. Give them a little taste in

RULE OF THUMB
Show, don't tell.

the presentation. Show them what's really on offer here—your skills!

Another important issue to think about is the "leave behind." Many presenters create and give the presentation in PowerPoint and then automatically give out the presentation to the audience as a bound book when they're done. Does anybody ever look at it again? It's doubtful. Giving out your entire presentation is a waste. Give out only those parts of the presentation (or alternative supporting materials) that back up the key points of your presentation. If your process is key, hand out your process chart—and nothing else. If the key is your design and experience, leave the client with a portfolio of your work, a brochure, or qualifications document that describes your relevant experience in detail. Select your leave-behind materials carefully: If you give out one piece of paper, they may actually look at it later; if you give out pounds of materials, they'll probably never open it.

BRIGHT IDEA
Instead of looking to new technology to make points with your audience, impress them with a paper and pen.

Rehearsing: How Do You Prepare for the Show?

You have to rehearse. You've spent hours planning your presentation and creating materials. Now you have to figure out what you're going to say, and you have to practice saying it. Many architects are very casual about rehearsals, either because they obsess over their materials, don't build enough time for rehearsal into the process, don't know how to rehearse, or don't see a benefit to rehearsal. Too many architects, having slaved over materials for days, walk into the presentation cold, unprepared, and try to play it by ear. If you rehearse, you may just look like you know what you're talking about when you open your mouth to talk. If you don't rehearse, you risk looking unprepared (even though you spent a week on that org chart), as if you don't know your own material (no matter how well you do), and unprofessional.

There are a lot of excuses for not preparing. Some people who don't know how to prepare for a presentation will claim, "I don't rehearse. I'm much fresher when I start a presentation without rehearsing. Rehearsal makes me flat." Running through what you're going to say once or twice makes you lose your spark? Get serious. You'll certainly be fresh if you make up your presentation on the spot. But when the stakes are as high as your next project, wouldn't you rather actually know what you're going to say before you start talking?

Everybody prepares in his or her own way. One legendary architect approaches group rehearsal as a joke-writing session; he knows what he's going to say, but he frames and punctuates his sections of the presentation with jokes that he writes and tries out on the team in rehearsal. Whatever works for you, works for you.

If you're not quite a master presenter yet (and very few people are), and you don't quite know how to rehearse for a presentation, give this process a try:

1. *Know your part.* Circulate the agenda and copies of your presentation materials and ask everybody on the team to figure out what they're going to say.

2. *Schedule time to rehearse.* Find a time for everybody to meet and rehearse. Plan a rehearsal session that is at least two to three times as long as the actual presentation. Figure out who is going to direct the rehearsal.

TIP

Rehearsal will give you a command of your material and more confidence when speaking.

3. *Get everybody together, and focus.* Start the meeting on time. Stop work on anything other than getting your brain ready for the presentation. Put your pencils down; stop revising that org chart.

4. *Talk through it.* The "director" (whoever is running the rehearsal) should talk through the presentation, step by step, reviewing who is going to present which sections. This is the time for discussion. This is your last chance to change anything.

5. *Run through it.* Get up and go. Run through the presentation at about half-energy, but go through the motions fully. If you're going to show a board, show the board. If you're going to stand up, stand up. Don't stop: Really try to simulate the actual presentation, albeit at a lower energy level. Interrupt each other only if something is very wrong and needs to be fixed immediately. During the run-through, the entire presentation team should watch each presenter attentively, in order to discuss the presentation later.

6. *Notes.* When the run-through is over, talk about it. What worked? What didn't? Did you hit your points? Was the message clear? Did it flow? Are there any parts of the presentation that could be clearer?

7. *Fly through it again.* Do it again. This time, at a slightly higher energy level, and somewhat more focused. If you're running out of time, pick up your pace to faster than natural speed, without skipping a thing.

It is absolutely true that you can overrehearse for a presentation. If you're bored with your material, your audience will be bored with you. Don't run through the presentation a dozen times; work as long

RULE OF THUMB

Don't allow surprises during your presentation to get in your way. Plan your staging and transitions in rehearsal.

Presentations: The Chemistry Test

as what you're talking about is still interesting to you, and not a second longer. Save some spark for the actual presentation. This spark can come from anywhere—from the honest energy and chemistry of the presentation team, from your passion for the project, from your enthusiasm for your work, or from interaction with the client. Don't rehearse to the point at which you're sick of talking about the project and your work. If you need to, find ways to make rehearsal interesting for yourself—try it a different way, try it without materials or with different materials, anything to keep the process alive and to save some passion for the actual presentation to the client.

Presentation Tips and Tricks: Do's and Don'ts

There's a lot more to say about the art and science of preparing and delivering a blowout presentation. But as the focus of this book is much broader than this subject, this discussion needs to be abbreviated. To close this chapter, here are a few additional tips to help you make persuasive marketing presentations:

▶ *Make it interactive.* Whether you're presenting to 3 people or 300, find ways to engage your audience and make them do something. If your presentation consists of you talking for 90 minutes, you're dead. Make your audience talk, ask them questions, get them to stand up, anything to get them involved.

▶ *Use stories to make your point.* Storytelling is an incredibly effective means of communication. Stories can make your material interesting and relevant to an audience and can help them remember what you're talking about. Practice telling stories.

► *Risk Equals Reward.* Take a chance; it usually pays off. Don't play it safe. If you have ideas about the project, work them into your presentation. If you're pretty sure about how the project needs to go, say it. Biting your tongue and giving a safe presentation isn't going to impress the client; having breakthrough ideas just might. The client may not agree with everything you say, but your passion and inspiration will shine through.

► *Use familiar materials.* Whenever possible, try to present material that you're personally familiar with and have a personal connection to. If you work for a big firm, you may be in the position of presenting past experience that is not your own. That's fine; but present your own projects whenever possible. Experience comes alive when it's personal.

► *Skills are important.* Get some training! If you want to look like you know what you're doing when you get up in front of an audience to speak, get some presentation training! Presentation skills can make the difference between looking polished and looking awkward in front of a group. There are lots of great presentation training consultants. Hire one to do a two-day training session for a dozen or so key presenters in your firm. At the very least, read David Greusel's fine book on the topic of presentation skills (part of this series), *The Architect's Essentials of Presentation Skills* (John Wiley & Sons, Inc., 2002).

- *Invite an audience to your rehearsal.* On your second run-through, invite one or more experienced presenters into your rehearsal to watch and critique your performance. It may seem hard to expose yourself to criticism, but if you can do it, it can dramatically improve your presentation.

- *Anticipate questions.* Think about your weaknesses. Prepare for questions that the audience to the presentation may ask you. You don't want the client to ask you anything that comes as a surprise. Do your research about the client, the project, and the competition, and discuss any potential liabilities that you have. Make a list of tough questions that the client may ask you about your firm, your experience, or your proposal, and have answers ready.

- *Follow up.* While you're in the presentation, think about your follow-up. Is there any additional information that you can send the client? Is there anything that you can say in a follow-up letter to reinforce your key points? When you get back to your desk from the presentation, immediately write a letter thanking the client for the opportunity to present. Include any additional information that may help the client's decision. Get the letter to the client as soon as you can—the same day, if at all possible. Call in two days, if you haven't heard anything.

Most important, remember that the presentation is a chemistry test. It's all about you, about whether the client likes you and can trust you. Your materials and your content are important insofar as they give the client reasons to believe that you are competent and trustworthy. But it isn't about the materials, and it isn't about your firm. When you're presenting, it's about you, and little else.

Design Competitions
High Risk and High Impact

10

Design competitions present a significant challenge for most architectural firms. To win a competition requires innovation, determination, a tremendous amount of hard work, and at least a little luck. At the same time, design competitions are incredibly speculative endeavors; even if the competition is compensated, the fees rarely come close to matching the amount of time and effort that the competition requires. So when a design competition is announced for an important new project, most firms have a real dilemma: answer the challenge, throwing time and energy into the competition and taking a financial risk, or don't enter and give up any chance of winning the project. It's like the lottery: You can't win if you don't enter—except that a competition will cost you a lot more than a dollar and a dream. Often it takes six figures and weeks or months of work.

Of course, competitions aren't just about winning or losing; there can be benefits to entering even if you don't win. Depending on the project, you may be able to use your competition proposal to build your portfolio, especially if you're a finalist. Many firms view competitions as a way to keep their creative juices flowing between projects that may not be as creative or exciting. Competitions can also be an opportunity to give junior staff a chance to participate actively in the design process.

Among architectural firms, there are three prevailing attitudes toward competitions:

> *Competitions are a waste of time and money. We never enter.* Some firms recognize that their odds of winning, combined with the high cost, make competitions a losing proposition in every case.

> *We enter competitions rarely and with great caution.* Other firms believe that they can, occasionally, beat the odds and win a competition, and that the benefits of winning in terms of portfolio building, media coverage, and/or compensation are worth the risk. The competition effort needs to be managed carefully to limit the firm's losses.

> *Competitions are a valuable part of our marketing efforts. We enter them frequently.* There are also firms that consider competitions an irreplaceable part of their firm strategy. These are generally small design firms that are looking for an edge over their competitors. They believe that the level playing field of a design competition gives them a chance to show their stuff and sometimes beat out entrenched competitors.

Most firms seem to be in the middle category, entering competitions only occasionally, and tending to spend much more time and money on the competition than they ever get back. There are only a few firms in the United States that repeatedly and consistently win profitable work from competitions. (Firms such as Weiss/Manfredi, Diller+Scofidio, and Eisenman Architects come to mind.) It's different in Europe, where competitions are a much more common way to hire an architect and are an indispensable part of the marketing efforts of many European architectural firms.

Types of Competitions: Open, Invited, and Informal

There are several different ways that sponsoring organizations set up competitions to select architects. Organizations may elect to make a competition open to anyone or only to an invited group of firms, or they may insert a competition in a conventional selection process to see how competing firms approach a design challenge. The key types of competitions are as follows:

- ➤ *Open.* The competition is advertised in architectural publications or even the newspaper. The barriers to entry are reasonably low. Not every entrant will be compensated, but frequently the finalists are.

- ➤ *Invited.* The competition sponsor will select a limited group of architectural firms to participate in the competition. This selection is sometimes made through a qualifications process, in which a larger group of firms is invited to submit qualifications packages. The firms that are invited to compete often receive a fixed amount of compensation for their entry.

- ➤ *Informal.* Sometimes an organization that is undertaking a project and going through the architect selection process decides to hold an informal competition so they can compare the design abilities of the competing firms. The organization asks a number of architects who are under consideration to "show us your ideas." The firms may get a few weeks, or even a weekend, to put some drawings together before their presentation. The firms are not generally compensated for their work, but may be able to recoup the expense if they are hired for the project.

There are a number of publications in which a sponsoring organization may advertise an open competition or the qualifications stage of an invited competition. The quarterly publication *Competitions Magazine* features competition listings as well as the results of completed competitions. Competitions may also be advertised in the architectural press, in trade publications, in government contract reporting publications, or even in the newspaper.

Deciding to Enter the Competition: Be Sure before You Start

When you're considering pursuing a project that involves a design competition, the go/no-go decision process (see Chapter 8) is critical. You're about to put a considerable amount of money and effort on the line. Before you jump headlong into design, consider the following questions:

- ➤ What are our reasons for wanting to enter?
- ➤ Who has been invited to compete (if it's not an open competition)?
- ➤ Will we be compensated for entering?
- ➤ Who is on the competition jury?
- ➤ Is the competition blind? (Will the jury know who we are when they see our entry?)
- ➤ What will it cost us (in time and money) to prepare the entry?

- What are our real odds of winning?
- How badly do we want this project?
- Can we spare the staff time required?

The decision to compete in a design competition can be a very hard one to make. It can be difficult to objectively evaluate your odds of winning and to determine how much you're willing to lose. You're gambling, and it's not a small amount of money you're playing with. If you win, you can probably recoup your investment, but what if you lose?

Deciding to compete is a business decision. You need to balance your instincts and your passion for the project with a realistic look at the odds and the financials. Do you think you can win? What's it going to cost? How much are you willing to risk? There are certainly limits to how much you can reasonably spend that will determine how often you can pursue competitions and how many you can lose.

Many firms seem to be lax with their competition go/no-go decision process, and then don't always manage the design process as efficiently as they could. The result is that firms often spend more money and time on the competition than they had anticipated.

Your Competition Strategy: Taking a Risk and Making It Count

Assuming you've decided to pursue that design competition for the new student center, or the new office building, or the new master plan for that European city, what's your strategy for competing? How do you maximize your chances of winning the big prize?

Common architectural wisdom says that the way to win a competition is to break the rules, but it's not

TIP

Be very selective about pursuing competitions, and manage the process carefully to minimize your losses.

REMINDER

Include an allowance for competitions in your marketing budget.

clear that the evidence supports this idea. It's true that if you break the rules, your entry will stand out, and it may even display some level of increased passion or vibrancy; but dismissing the parameters of the competition is risky and may disqualify you, especially if the competition parameters you're flaunting exist in order to make the project feasible—such as budget and size constraints.

Here are a few basic tips to help you develop a strategy for the competition:

- ► *Listen.* Read the competition guidelines carefully. This may be all the information you get from the competition sponsor, so you have to make sure to absorb it all.

- ► *Study the context.* If the project has a designated site, visit it and review it. Research its history. Learn the neighborhood: What's next door and down the street? How is the project going to fit in with what's already there?

- ► *Be yourself.* This is a design competition. For once, it's a marketing exercise that is not (just) a popularity contest. You'll, hopefully, be judged on your abilities and the quality of the solution you propose. If there's a time to create something that comes from your heart and brings everything you have to offer to it, this is it.

- ► *Define the problem for yourself.* What do you think this project is really about? What's the real challenge here? What are the constraints within which the design solution needs to exist? What problems can this project solve?

- ► *Take a risk.* This is not the time to play it safe. Big ideas and strong voices win competitions. Make a statement with your proposal. Be bold.

- *Find a big idea.* Find something to unify your proposal, and relate everything to it in some way. Whether it's a design motif, a concept, a contextual element, a purpose for the project, an aesthetic, a feeling, an image, choose some big central idea and stick to it. It doesn't need to be applied rigidly; it can be like a theme floating through the project. But a strong central idea is essential.

- *Blow out the stops.* You've decided to go after this and you're in the competition to win it. Compromise is not an effective strategy at this point. You've got to do everything you can to win this competition. Go for broke.

Most of all, make sure that the competition reflects your firm's strategy, in terms of your choice to pursue it, your process, and your design solution. When you're deep in the competition process, it can be easy to forget the big picture and throw all of your energy into the design process. Try to maintain perspective, and create a proposal that reflects who you are as an architect and as a firm.

Managing the Competition— and Not Losing Your Shirt in the Process

Competitions present a management challenge. When the stakes are so high and the pressure is intense, how do you manage the process so that you spend an acceptable amount of time and money on your entry? Here are a few ideas:

1. *Have a budget.* Before you begin work on the competition, decide how much you're prepared to spend. Break it down in terms of staff

time and expenses. Make sure that the design team buys into the budget and agrees to work within it.

2. *Have a work plan.* Plan very carefully who is going to work on the competition and how much time each person is going to spend. Just as if you're working for a client, prepare a schedule for the competition that indicates critical milestones and internal review points. Stick to it.

3. *Track everything.* You need to know how much the competition is costing you, so nothing can slip by. Even if you're not compensating employees for overtime, track their hours anyway. Track every interim plot, every print. Be diligent about your expenses just as if this were a billable project for a client.

4. *Find a way to recoup your losses.* Face up to how much you're spending on the competition and find a way to justify the expense. If you win, make sure that the total cost of competition is recouped by your compensation for the project. If you lose, consider carefully what the benefits of competing were—staff experience, portfolio-building (can you use your competition entry as relevant experience for other clients/projects?), sharpening your "design teeth," and so on.

After the competition process is over, and you know how much you spent and what the outcomes were, take a moment to evaluate the process and reconsider your competition strategy. Given your experience with this process, how many competitions are reasonable to pursue in a given year? How many do you have to win in order to justify the expense? Most important, how do you feel about the process of working on your competition entry? Was it worthwhile? What were the benefits of working on the entry that did not relate to winning or losing? Can you use the competition proposal in your portfolio? Did the staff find the process valuable? Are you proud of the result? Learn from this process and allow it to inform your strategy for future competitions.

Closing the Deal
Setting the Fee, Negotiating, and Signing the Contract

There's a lot that happens between submitting your proposal or making your presentation and starting to work on the project. It can take weeks for the client to reach consensus on which firm to hire, negotiate with the preferred firm, and complete the internal process to have the contract prepared and approved. In that time, there's a lot that you can do besides sitting on your hands and waiting for the client to get back to you.

After the presentation, many firms just sit and wait—"Have they called yet?" "No, but they will!" Eventually, a fax or letter shows up that says that another firm has been selected. The letter gets filed. On to the next proposal . . .

Even though each member of the audience makes his or her own decision as to which firm to select, the firm that is chosen is not always the top choice of the majority of the audience. What really happens is far more complex, and is completely different from client to client and project to project. After the presentations are over, the internal negotiating and consensus building begins. Who should we hire? Who did you think was the best? It isn't generally put to a vote; it is discussed and decided based on the usual idiosyncratic decision-making process of the client organization. Generally, the loudest voices with the strongest opinions have a disproportionate influence on the selection, but the ultimate decision is made by the person of the highest authority. Sometimes, the internal politics on the client side can be more important in selecting an architect than the specific qualifications, capabilities, or proposed compensation of any of the candidates. Sometimes the results of the selection process can be surprising, even to some of those who were involved.

Your job isn't done when the presentation is over. You can't just walk out of the room and wait for a phone call. You've got work to do. You've got to try to influence the behind-closed-doors decision-making process by any means necessary. You've got to make sure that the client is going to pick your firm for this project.

What can you do?

> *Send a thank-you note.* It's so easy, it means so much, and so few people do it. As soon as you get back to the office from the presentation, fire off a quick thank-you note. Use it to reinforce your position in the client's mind by reiterating points from the presentation or by providing additional information on questions that the client had. Be gracious and be confident. A thank-you note is incredibly helpful in cementing the impression that you left in the interview. It shows that you are enthusiastic and polite.

> *Call the client.* Give it three days, then call the client. Thank them (again) for the interview and ask if a decision has been made yet. If not,

TIP

Let them know that you're still thinking about them, even after the presentation is over.

REMINDER

Few people write thank-you notes. By doing so, you will stand out as enthusiastic and caring.

ask whether they know when a decision will be made. Find a way to assert your enthusiasm for this project and for working with this client. Ask if there's any other information you can provide at this point. A call shows that you're interested, that you're serious, and that you're professional. It's also a point of personal contact that you can use to build your burgeoning relationship with the client.

► *Call third-party contacts.* Work your network. If you and the client have friends in common, call them and ask them to put in a good word for you. If there's a consultant or contractor who is involved in the process, call them and ask if they have any insight and if they could find out how it's going for you. Don't be pushy, but communicate how genuinely enthusiastic you are to work with this client.

► *Provide additional valuable information.* If you can, provide the client with information that may be valuable to them with regard to their project. If you have knowledge of the project that they might not have (about the site or code or legislation that might affect the project), send it to the client. This keeps you in mind and shows that you're thinking about the project.

► *Be patient.* Don't overdo it. Don't pester the client. Don't pester third parties. Once you've sent your thank-you note and called a few days later, find a way to offer the client something with each additional contact—information about the project or something else that's appropriate based on your relationship and your knowledge of the client.

➤ *Listen for hesitation and be prepared to adjust course.*
When you talk to the client, listen for any hesitation, any indication that the decision process
is not proceeding smoothly or that you may not
be the client's choice. Probe for anything that
you can do to get back on track. Is the proposal
right? Is the fee appropriate? Are there any
doubts on the client's side? Be prepared to sug-
gest altering your proposal if that's what it will
take.

If you detect resistance or doubt on the client's
part, try to interpret what that could mean. It may
not necessarily indicate that another firm has been
selected instead of yours. It might be that the project
is in trouble, or being rethought, or that there are
internal issues at the client's organization that are
getting in the way. Try to figure it out and reposition
your approach so that your firm is still the right
choice.

When You Lose: Find Out Why and Fix It

No matter what you do, you may still lose. It happens. Losing isn't fun, so most people just want to
put the experience behind them as quickly as possible. While this may be healthy from a psychological
point of view, when you move on too quickly, you
miss a real opportunity to find out what the client
really thought about you, to learn what you can do to
improve, and to build an ongoing relationship with
the client that may lead to work at some point down
the road.

When you find out you've lost, always express
your disappointment, then ask why. You may ini-

tially get an off-the-shelf answer: "Your fee was too high." "The other firm had more experience." But by now, from reading this book, you know this isn't how selection decisions are made, so don't let it go with that. Let the client know that you really want to learn what you can do to improve for next time, and that you're committed to building a long-term relationship with the client and working together eventually. Ask if they would mind meeting and talking about the process and what you could have done better. You're asking for a favor here, so ask nicely. The client doesn't have to meet with you, doesn't have to give you any information except "No, thanks." But if you're humble and express a sincere desire to improve, it would be a hard-hearted client (or a bureaucrat) that would turn you down.

TIP

When you lose a project, it's a great opportunity to start to build a relationship with the client.

When you meet with the client, try to get a truly honest assessment of what the client thought of your firm, your proposal, your presentation. You're coming to the client to learn. You don't want them to respect your feelings; you want their honest perceptions. Put them at ease; ask probing questions; ask how you compared to the competition; ask why you lost; ask what the competition did to put them over the edge. Take anything they'll give you. Learn from what they say, make adjustments, and don't repeat your mistakes.

TIP

When you lose, always try to find out why. Ask for a "debriefing" meeting with the client.

As stated throughout this book, the secret to marketing (if it can be called a secret at all) is people. Your ability to build and maintain relationships with people is more important to your marketing success than anything else. This meeting with this client, at a time when you aren't selling anything, is a great time to build your relationship. The client is doing you a favor, and, hopefully, the client's guard is down.

This is a person with whom you can form a friendship, or at least a sociable business relationship. As you meet, and learn from your mistakes, look for an opportunity to make ongoing contact with this client. What do you have in common? Is there information that you can you provide to the client (articles, etc.) as the project proceeds?

Negotiating the Deal: Where to Give In and Where to Stand Firm

The client invites you to a meeting to negotiate your contract. You think you've won the project. You go to the meeting and the client asks you to lower your fee. What do you do? Do you lower your fee in order to make sure you get the job or do you hold firm to your original proposal and risk blowing it?

Your answer will to some extent depend on the client's attitude and your strategy. How badly do you want this project? How serious does the client seem? If you're a high-profile design firm and you know that the client wants to hire you for the project, your negotiating position can be very different than if you know that you came out slightly ahead in a competition of firms that are perceived as equals.

If a client asks to negotiate your fee or some other point of your contract, remember that your fee is based on many factors. To change one factor should imply a change in compensation, and lowering your compensation should imply that some other factor has to shift. Never negotiate just your fee; negotiate your entire service offering, including your fee. The negotiation can include any or all of these factors:

TIP

Enter with a positive attitude. Negotiating is not about giving in, but about finding common ground.

- *Services provided.* The more services you propose to provide, the more it should cost.

- *Project area.* The more expansive the project, the more expensive the fee.

- *Team.* The best professionals cost more. Your fee is based on the individuals that you have proposed to work on the project.

- *Schedule.* Completing the project exactly when the client wants it may cost more.

- *Quality.* It's tough to define design quality, but your proposal assumes a certain level of quality. Is there a way to adjust this assumption and to offer a lower fee for a lower level of quality, or to raise your fee to accommodate a higher level of quality?

- *Risk.* By engaging in an agreement to complete this project, both you and the client are taking on risk. The client is putting money on the line; you're putting your reputation and labor on the line. Is there a way to negotiate this risk, reducing risk for either of you in exchange for movement on some other issue?

- *Contract terms.* Every term in the contract is negotiable, including payment terms, insurance, and those "what happens in case something goes wrong" provisions.

When you begin negotiations with a client, your attitude is critical. You have a choice about how you approach the process, and this attitude can determine the success of the outcome. Too often, architects put themselves in a weak position, and will sign just about anything that is offered in order to get the work. In other cases, they approach negotiation as an adversarial process, trying to hold on to their

FOR MORE INFORMATION

Read *Getting to Yes*, by Roger Fisher and William Ury, which proposes that negotiation can be a collaborative, rather than adversarial, process of finding common ground.

TIP

Be honest and forthcoming about your requirements.

TIP

Always have a lawyer work with you to iron out contract terms.

position (or even improve their position) without giving anything up.

Negotiation doesn't need to be adversarial, or a process that you've lost before you even walk into the room. Negotiation is an interpersonal process. You have a personal relationship (or are building one) with your new client. Negotiating is about working together to find common ground between you and your client, and discovering options that work for both of you. The key is communication that is objective in nature. You need to listen to the client's issues, and to state yours clearly. Then you need to work together to find solutions to these issues that work for all concerned.

Whatever you do, don't just automatically sign whatever agreement is presented in order to get the work. Work with a lawyer on the agreement to make sure that the terms are acceptable to you. When you sign an agreement with unfavorable terms, you're aren't just potentially hurting your own firm, you're also setting a precedent for other firms and for the terms that the architectural profession is willing to accept in general. Architects are, to some extent, in this together; it's important to the profession that you only agree to terms that are fair.

If you're looking for a starting point for negotiating an agreement with your client, consider using the AIA's standard forms for agreements between owner and architect. The agreements include terms that have been developed by the AIA to be acceptable to architects. There are many forms to choose from, depending on the project (B141, B155, B171, etc.). They are available from your local AIA chapter or online.

Delivering on Your Promises: Following Through and Checking Back

You've won the project and signed the contract. Now it's showtime: You have to deliver on your promises. You may feel like the hard part is over and that it's downhill from here. However, the stakes, and the client's expectations, are higher than ever. Your reputation is on the line. Your brand as an architectural firm is determined not by how you win work, but how you do the work. The client selected you from a field of competitors because they believed that you were the best choice for the job. You can't let them down.

It's important to manage your client's expectations from the start of the project so that they know what to expect from the design process. The client will judge you not in terms of some objective criteria of design and performance, but in terms of their own expectations. You have to be explicit with the client about what they can expect from you—when you'll deliver what, what the process will be, how you'll work together, what it will cost, how long it will take, and so on. Don't allow anything about the process to be unclear in the client's mind, or an unrealistic expectation (or a bad impression of you) may result. Communicate often with the client, both verbally and in writing, and always prep them for what the next steps are.

Once you've told the client what they can expect and what happens next, you have to make sure your team follows through. Take a good look at your team. Is what you've promised feasible for them? Is it a challenge or something they've done a thousand times before? Do you have any concerns at all about their ability to deliver what the client expects? Communicate the client's expectations to the team clearly: what the client wants, when they want it, what the important issues are. Strive to create a culture in your firm that makes the client the focus of all of your efforts, and that favors open communication and professionalism (doing what you say you are going to do, behaving in a "professional" manner, etc.). By doing so, your job of delivering the project in a manner acceptable to the client will be a lot easier.

While you're working on the project, check back with the client frequently to see how they are feeling about your work and the project in general. Foster a communicative relationship in which the client can tell you openly how the project is progressing. Listen to what the client has to say. If there's a problem, fix it immediately. Alter course if necessary (to change the team, rethink the schedule, etc.), but keep the client happy.

You're closer to the client now than you've ever been. Take the opportunity to transform your business relationship into a friendship; take the client to lunch, have a drink, play golf—do something social. The closer you are as individuals, the easier it will be to communicate about issues on the project and the better you'll be perceived. Your relationship (and the client's perception of your firm) will also be invaluable when the client is considering architects for the next project.

Once the project is complete, plan how you will check back to see how the client is doing and how the project that you designed for them is working. Plan to call the client every three months for the first year

TIP

Open communication helps you avoid unpleasant surprises.

TIP

In dealing with clients in the public sector, you may have to play according to a slightly different set of rules (e.g., you might have lunch with a government worker, but you probably won't be able to pick up the tab). Make sure you know what the rules are for the specific agency you're dealing with.

Closing the Deal

after the project is finished. When you call, ask honestly and openly how the project is working out for them and whether there have been any problems. Learn from what the client tells you. If appropriate, offer solutions to the client, and offer to help implement them.

Depending on the project, you may want to consider conducting a more formal *postoccupancy evaluation* six months or a year after project completion. A postoccupancy evaluation is a survey that goes to people who may be working in or using the new facility. Depending on the questions you ask, you can gain valuable insight, not only into how the facility holds up, but into how people use the facility, how people feel about, and how it's changed their lives.

If you're in frequent contact with the client, and the client has a favorable impression of you, your firm, and the work you've done together, the client should give you indications about additional opportunities with their organization. Whatever you do, don't push it. You're here to help, not to sell them additional services. Engage in a friendly conversation about what's going on with them, listen for additional opportunities, offer advice, and ask if you can help. If you've done a good job so far, there's no reason why the client should say no. And you've built an enduring client relationship based on trust and respect that can contribute to your firm's success for years to come.

Marketing Tools and Resources
Your Arsenal of Marketing Weapons

Part

III

I n working to build their business and bring in work, many firms get caught on a marketing treadmill: get lead, receive RFP, respond to RFP, make presentation. Break yourself out of the same repetitive cycle. Recognize that you have an entire arsenal of marketing weapons, most of which you probably never use. Do you have a thorough internal communications program? Do you take full advantage of the client communications opportunities? Are you doing as much as you can in the area of media relations? Do you have the right marketing staff and consultants? There's always more that you can do to increase your impact. It isn't just about proposals.

This part includes eight chapters, each of which highlights a different marketing tool or set of tools. Most of us don't realize how many tools we have at our disposal. Use them, and watch how much more successful you can be!

- ► *Chapter 12—Research: Obtaining Market Intelligence*
- ► *Chapter 13—Knowledge Management: Systems for Tracking Information*
- ► *Chapter 14—Internal Communications: Getting the Message to Your Staff*
- ► *Chapter 15—Client Communications: Newsletters, Web Sites, Direct Mail, Advertising, and Events*

Research
Obtaining Market Intelligence

12

When most people think of market research, they think of surveys and focus groups. They think of those people who call you on the phone, ask you about what kind of gum you chew, and, if you're lucky, invite you to a focus group where they pay you to tell them what you think about the gum.

In the world of product marketing, this is exactly what market research is: a primary research technique utilizing focus groups, direct-mail surveys, and personal interviews to find out about customer demographics and preferences. In fact, market research is a $5 billion a year industry. Product companies hire research companies to do market tests, make calls, run focus groups, and conduct Web surveys to find out how their existing products are doing and if their new products will work in the real world—before they spend millions on mass production and marketing.

Research is a very different thing in the design industry. Whereas product companies need to do a lot of market research because their products are often invented, developed, distributed, and sold with little direct contact between the manufacturer and the user, design firms, as service providers, are in constant contact with their clients. As an architect, it's your job to know your clients and to understand their needs. And because you hear what your clients need directly from them, you are, essentially, doing primary research all the time.

Research is the process of acquiring information and making it relevant to your business, turning it into intelligence that you can use to make informed decisions. Any time you actively gather information, you're conducting research. It doesn't have to be formal or planned. Cocktail party conversations are as valid a form of research as reading obscure journal articles—especially if they provide you with timely intelligence.

Research can help you in many different ways:

▶ Understand your clients—who they are, what their issues are.

▶ Identify new potential markets and opportunities.

▶ Understand the big picture to make informed decisions about your business.

▶ Learn what your competitors are doing, your position in the marketplace, and what makes you different.

▶ Validate your methods and beliefs.

▶ Figure out how you can improve your process (both marketing and delivery).

You can research anything that you want to know more about or understand better. Here are a few possible topics:

▶ Your firm (what you need to work on or worry about)

▶ Existing clients (research doesn't stop when you get the job)

TIP

Keep your ears open! You could be doing research while boarding a plane, getting coffee, or visiting a friend.

- Potential clients (who they are, what their goals are, what they're looking for)
- Your competitors
- Existing/potential markets, defined by geography, industry, service, and project type (for trends, issues, growth, opportunity)
- Government activity (with regard to how new laws will affect your businesses, etc.)
- Broad societal trends (such as rethinking suburban sprawl and how this will affect development in the United States)

Research is a continuous process. You're doing it all the time by talking to people and reading the newspaper and trade publications. But aside from your daily informal research that you do on the phone or around the water cooler, sometimes you need to conduct more extensive research to get a more complete picture of the deeper issues surrounding a subject—such as when you're contemplating an organizational change (name, ownership, acquisition, relocation) or entering a new market.

TIP

Research can help you make informed business choices.

Research can be described as either primary or secondary, and either qualitative or quantitative (see the illustration on the next page).

Primary Research: From the Horse's Mouth

Primary research is research you conduct yourself or hire someone else to do for you, such as surveying your clients. You're in direct contact with your research subject—you decide what the format of the research is going to be and what questions you're going ask. Primary research can include everything from taking a contact to lunch to learn about a

TYPES OF RESEARCH

	QUANTITATIVE	QUALITATIVE
PRIMARY	**NUMBER CRUNCHING** 74% OF SURVEY RESPONDERS WOULD HIRE US AGAIN	**OPINIONS, RUMORS** THEY SAID WE NEED TO IMPROVE OUR DELIVERY
SECONDARY	**FACTS AND FIGURES** THE TOTAL SIZE OF THAT MARKET IS $3 BILLION	**GENERAL INFORMATION** YOU NEED A LICENSE TO WORK IN THAT MARKET

TIP

Take your client out for lunch—that's research!

project to engaging in a formal study to find out how your firm is perceived. Primary research is essential when you want to find out about your company's position in the marketplace: how your performance ranks with your competitors, how an organizational or image change will alter the perception of your firm, whether your marketing materials are effective, or how you did on your last job.

Primary research can include surveys, phone interviews, face-to-face interviews, or focus groups, or any other methods that provide you with first-hand information directly from somebody's mouth. The advantages of primary research are that it's usually focused and specific, highly relevant to your business needs, proprietary (in that your competitors will not have access to your information), and potentially relationship-building, in the sense that you may be interacting with your clients through the research. The disadvantages are that it's expensive and time-consuming; and, often, to do primary research right, you'll need to bring in a specialist from outside your firm who is objective and has the right skills.

You do primary research every day, and you can always do more. It's valuable to call a client you haven't talked to in a while just to ask how things are going. It's always helpful to ask your clients to review a new marketing program, to ask their opinion on a new corporate identity or a new brochure. It's a good idea to interview your clients after a project to find out what they felt about your performance and how they thought the project turned out.

Secondary Research: "I Read Somewhere That . . ."

Secondary research is research that already exists— that's published, that's online, that's in *The New York Times*. Thanks to the expanding availability and quantity of Internet resources, secondary research has become much easier and less expensive to conduct than in the past. Today, almost every publication has an online version, whereas before the Internet, you had to collect magazines, hire research agencies, go to the library. Now all you need is an Internet connection and maybe a login to a subscription-based search engine such as Lexis-Nexis or Dialog.

The advantages of secondary research are that it's readily available and relatively inexpensive. The disadvantages are that the information you find may be dated; the information may be not specific enough for your needs (geographic area or market too broadly defined, etc.); the data might be flawed or

 TIP

Encourage everyone to conduct informal secondary research. Buy office subscriptions to relevant industry and general-purpose publications.

biased; and any information you find is also available to your competitors.

Qualitative and Quantitative Research: The Soft and Hard of It

Basically, qualitative research is information—facts or opinions. Quantitative research is data, the hard numbers that support a position. Qualitative research is used to determine details, meanings, attitudes, facts. Quantitative research is used to fix exact quantities and make comparisons.

Sometimes quantitative research is used to determine and analyze the total opportunity in a new market—the total annual construction volume in China, for example. In other instances, quantitative research is conducted to provide validity to substantiate a position—for example, statistical assessment of client survey results to try to figure out whether to change your firm name when a partner leaves.

Aside from finding out information through networking (essentially primary research), much of the research that we do in our industry is qualitative and secondary. We use research to figure out who our prospective clients are and what the opportunities are in new markets. It's generally easy to find existing (secondary) information on topics like this—either through publications or on the Internet.

Research Methodology: Beyond Networking and Newspapers

Whatever your subject or research method, research is all about asking the right questions and listening for the answers. Let your inquisitiveness guide you:

Ask good questions and you'll come up with the answers.

Here's a basic 10-step approach to researching anything:

1. *Identify and state the issue.* What's your subject? What are you trying to find out?

2. *Specify research goals.* What do you expect? How far do you want to take the research?

3. *Determine the information requirements.* What kinds of information do you need?

4. *Determine your research method.* Primary or secondary? Surveys? Interviews? Web research?

5. *Decide on the research sample.* How many people will you talk to? How much reading will you do?

6. *Determine what to ask.* What are the specific questions you want to ask—whether you're asking survey respondents or asking yourself while you browse the Web?

7. *Develop questionnaire/survey/process.* Put your questions into the right form.

8. *Conduct research.* Distribute surveys, conduct interviews, search the Web.

9. *Document results and analyze.* Gather your information; begin to assess it.

10. *Produce report with findings.* Distill your findings into a format that you can share effectively with others.

The critical step, of course, is figuring out which questions to ask to find out what you'd like to know. To that end, let's consider a few types of research in detail: researching the perception of your company, researching a new market, and researching a new client or project.

Soul-Searching: Researching Your Company—How Are You Perceived in the Marketplace?

Sometimes you may want to research how your company is perceived in the marketplace. This research is especially valuable when you're contemplating a major change in your business, such as a name change, merger or acquisition, or leadership transition. Research at times like this enables you not only to find out how audiences perceive you, but also to test any change you're considering to see if you'll be perceived differently after the change.

When you consider researching how your firm is perceived, you have three major choices to make:

- ► Who conducts the survey? Consultants or in-house personnel?

- ► Do we use interviews or paper/online surveys? Personal or impersonal?

- ► Who do we interview/survey? Just clients or others in the marketplace?

If you're going through a major change, you may want to hire an outside consultant to help you with the research. Not only will the consultant be more familiar with research techniques, but someone from the outside will also be more objective and provide a more balanced analysis of the research results. Also, clients may be more open and frank with an interviewer who is perceived as being a "third party," rather than a member of your staff.

The choice of interviews or surveys will depend on what kinds of information you hope to receive. Surveys may be easier to conduct, but they are better suited to acquiring quantitative information than qualitative. People don't generally write in the blanks on surveys, unless they have a very strong opinion;

TIP

Clients may be more honest about your firm if they are talking to an objective listener, rather than a member of your staff.

Research: Obtaining Market Intelligence

usually they just check the boxes. Interviews are a more effective way to capture qualitative information, and are probably a better choice if you're trying to determine the answer to a qualitative question such as "how are we perceived?"

You'll also need to determine whom you're going to interview: Will it just be former clients, or will it include others in the industry (contractors, consultants, prospective clients, etc.)? This, again, will depend on your goals, whether you're trying to gauge your client base or get a broader sense of how you're perceived.

Whether you decide to do a survey or interviews, develop questions that are precise and targeted to exactly what you would like to know. Ask the same questions of every respondent. Here are a few sample questions:

- When you think of our firm, what pops into your head?
- Are there any negatives associated with us?
- How would you say that we compare with other firms?
- What do you think of our work? (open-ended or multiple choice)
- What could we improve?
- How satisfied were you with the results of the project? (multiple choice)
- How likely are you to work with us again? (multiple choice)
- What did you think of our proposal/presentation? (multiple choice)

When you ask questions like this, you need to be open to the results. You may not like all the answers, but those that are more difficult to hear or read are ultimately more valuable, as they point the way toward possible improvement.

Testing the Waters: Researching a New Market— New Industry, Facility Type, Service, or Geographic Area

Let's say you want to get into a new market sector. It could be a new industry (pharmaceuticals), facility type (data centers), service (landscape architecture), or geographic area (China). Whatever the market, a few of the many things that you may want to try and determine include the following:

- ► Total size of the opportunity: How big is the total market?

- ► Cost of entry: What do we have to do/know to work in this market?

- ► Target organizations/agencies: If we enter this market, what is our target audience?

- ► Potential competitors: Who is working in this market already?

- ► Special regulations: Are there any particular laws or standards of practice that govern this market?

- ► Financial expectations: Will this a profitable market? What are fees like?

- ► Potential partners: Who can help us? Are there consultants we can team with?

- ► Trends/projections: What's changing in this market?

This research is, ideally, both quantitative and qualitative, and is probably compiled from the Internet, periodicals, and other secondary sources. You may also want to investigate conducting some primary research, by interviewing people who have first-hand knowledge of this market.

Digging Deep: Researching a Prospective Client— Either Proactively or in Response to an Opportunity

When you've identified a client (company, institution, agency) as one that you'd like to work with, or when you've heard of a new opportunity for an organization you aren't familiar with, it is critical to your marketing effort that you know as much as possible about the prospective client, the business the client is in, and any relationship that you might have had with this client in the past. This information will enable you to figure out how to approach the client and, later, how to create the most appropriate proposal and/or presentation you can for this client, informed by an understanding of who they are, where they are, and where they're headed.

For any company, institution, or agency, there is far more information available than you probably need, therefore focus only on the information that will be useful to you. It probably isn't particularly important that you capture the company's quarterly gross and net incomes for the last five years, but it is important that you can understand the culture and vision of this client.

Here are a several sample questions to get you started:

> What industry are they in? What do they do?

> What is their mission? Why do they exist?

> What's their history?

> How big are they? (revenue/budget, staff, etc.)

> Where are they located?

> How much space do they have? Where?

TIP

Use your network to find people who can tell you more about a prospective market.

- Are they growing?
- Any big plans on the horizon?
- Who are their clients?
- Who are their competitors?
- What's their organizational structure? Who's in charge?
- What's their financial health/history?
- What are their contract terms? What is their credit rating? Do they pay their bills?
- Who works for them now?
- What's changing in their markets?
- Do we have an existing relationship with them?

If you're researching a prospective client in response to receiving an RFP or hearing about a specific lead, one of your top questions will certainly be: What's driving this project? Depending on the project, you may have many other questions about its context and requirements that you'll want to research.

This research is mostly secondary, on the Internet, but there could be a primary aspect to it as well (asking third parties what they know/think about the client). And it's probably mostly qualitative, with just a few quantitative facts—such as revenue/budget, projected growth, and the like.

The facts are important, but when you're targeting a company, institution, or agency, the most critical thing is to gain an understanding of who they are, what their culture is, what their essence is. Having a good sense of the organization is essential when you communicate with them—whether in a letter, proposal, or presentation.

Finally, remember that research is never finished. It's not something you do once and then forget about once you've won or lost the project. The world keeps turning. Stuff changes all the time. If you win the job, you have to stay up to date on what's going on with your client. You have to understand your client and their issues so you can continue to provide them with the services they need.

Online Research

Most secondary research today is Internet-based. When doing research on the Internet about a company, institution, or agency, consider the following sources of information:

➤ *The prospective client's Web site.* Great for general background information, but bear in mind it will necessarily be biased—you won't find much bad news or criticism on the client's own site.

➤ *Single-source proprietary research sites (Lexis-Nexis, Dialog, etc.).* These have tremendous amounts of published articles and government information, but often at a premium cost.

➤ Search engines (Yahoo!, Google, AltaVista, etc.). Use these to find out which sites on the Web mention the organization you're researching.

➤ *Web versions of newspapers, magazines, and other publications.* Check these to find out the latest news and any investigative reports about the prospective client.

➤ *Public records.* Here you'll find corporate registrations, patents/trademarks, lawsuits, and so on.

➤ *Phone books.* Open these to find locations and other contact information.

➤ *Insider sites* (e.g., Vault.com). Written by and for current/former/prospective employees, these sites can give you a sense of the culture of the prospective client.

Knowledge Management
Systems for Tracking Information

13

Knowledge management is vital to the success of your marketing efforts and your business. Knowledge management includes all the systems—whether electronic, physical, or procedural—that enable your staff to store, find, and utilize valuable information. The greatest database ever created won't help if your staff isn't invested in it and they don't put their information in it.

Knowledge management begins and ends with people. It's critical that you and staff organize and share information in a way that is natural and efficient to you. Databases and filing systems can help you, but you can't start with the filing system or database and expect organization to be the unavoidable result. You have to begin with an organization system that feels natural to you, then build systems to formalize the organization and communicate how information is to be captured and shared.

Knowledge management is a challenge for every company. Everyone struggles to find the balance between systems and human factors. How much information do you need to track? How much is too much? What's the best way to track it? You need to have all the right information, but if you create long complex forms to track your information, you may put people off with an onerous data collection process and end up with an empty database.

Some firms have cultures that more effectively support knowledge management than others. Knowledge management requires people to be comfortable freely sharing information with each other. If your firm has a culture in which, for whatever reason, people with knowledge are regarded as more important than those without it, and where people are not comfortable sharing their information, it's going to be very difficult to institute an effective knowledge-sharing system. Real estate brokers are notoriously bad at institutional knowledge management, because the professional success of a broker is predicated on the broker having information that his or her colleagues don't have.

If you can get it right, your knowledge management system can be a true differentiator between you and your competition. When a client asks you a question to which you don't personally know the answer, whether it's about one of the firm's past projects or which audiovisual consultants you work with, how long does it take you to find the answer? Do you need to ask a person, or can you find the answer in some easy-to-use electronic or physical resource? If you can find the right information quickly, you'll look much smarter to the client. Knowledge is power, after all.

Most firms use three different types of systems to store information: human, physical, and electronic. Here are the strengths and weaknesses of each:

> *Human (the information in your brain).* If it's in somebody's head, all you have to do is call that person to find the answer. But what happens if

the person with the answer leaves the firm, or retires, or is on vacation? Relying on people's brains for knowledge management is comfortable and natural, but it's also only as reliable as the people you have, and only works when you can reach them.

➤ *Physical (your files).* Many of us still think of information as existing on paper and being filed in folders and cabinets (that's why computer systems use the metaphor of folders to describe file locations). You need a way to file that paper so that you can find it again when you need it. Physical files are comfortable and easily scalable, but they require office "real estate," and the more files you have, the more the system becomes a black hole: information goes in, but you never want to dig in there to bring it out.

➤ *Electronic (databases, file systems).* As we get better at creating databases, and more comfortable trusting the information we put in them, we capture more and more knowledge from our heads and our paper files to put in databases and electronic file systems. The difficulty is in creating electronic systems that feel natural and that aren't overly onerous to update and maintain. When these systems are executed efficiently, the advantages are many: instant access to information, easy sharing of information, access to information from anywhere in the world via the Internet, and low physical space requirements.

Think about all the different kinds of information your company needs to capture and maintain—on your projects as well as in areas related to finance, legal, human resources, and marketing. We'll talk briefly about five different types of information necessary for marketing and for which firms need to develop management systems: research, leads, people, projects, and staff.

Research: Trends, Articles, White Papers

You're collecting information all the time. Much of it doesn't fit into neat little categories, but it relates to your work, your markets, and your projects in ways that are difficult to track. When you find an article in the newspaper that talks about a client you're working for or an organization you'd like to work for, what do you do with it? Where do you put it so you can find it again? When you find information that relates to your practice, on sustainable design or the future of healthcare architecture, where does it go?

TIP

Research is a constant process, and your knowledge management system must be able to keep up.

Research is difficult to store and track because it's free-form information. It doesn't fit (usually) into a database, because the information can't be separated into neat fields that can be searched later. Another challenge is that this information can appear in lots of different formats, mostly on paper: newspaper and magazine articles, white papers, notes.

For the most part, research information usually exists in people's heads, supported by physical files of articles and other information. When you're looking for trends or specific information, you want to talk to an expert. It's tough to take the expert out of the process, and to automate a complex data retrieval process.

To support the marketing efforts of your firm, you need to create a system for storing research and other information that relates to the work of your firm. Start with an empty physical file and an empty electronic file. Fill each with appropriate information that you find or that comes your way: articles, Web links, other information. As you get it, segment and organize the information in ways that are logical to you, forming a system for organization and retrieval. Don't force it—don't overorganize the system; provide just enough organization so that you can find what you're looking for, but not so much that you're a slave to it. As your physical and electronic research files grow, they will become increasingly valuable resources to you and the staff of your firm.

Leads: Managing Information Down the Marketing Pipeline

TIP

Keep it comfortable. If organizing becomes more of a chore than an aid, you'll stop doing it.

In order to manage your business development process, you have to find a way to track opportunities as you develop them from leads to prospects to projects. Some firms use customizable off-the-shelf systems to do this, while others develop their own systems. Some just use a spreadsheet, such as Microsoft Excel, to track their leads.

If you're considering buying a system to track leads, you have to understand the lingo and the available options. Lead-tracking software is commonly referred to as *client* (or *customer*) *relationship management systems*, or CRMs. More specifically, some providers refer to their systems as *sales automation software*.

There are many systems out there, none of which are designed just for architects. However, a few are specific to our industry, and can be used by architects, engineers, construction firms, and related consultants. Deltek and Cosential are two industry-specific providers of lead-tracking and other software. There is a much wider choice of CRM software that is not specific to our industry, but that has been developed to provide sales automation for people doing sales in any industry. The challenge with using sales automation software that is not industry-specific is that this software will probably need to be customized to track information that is important to architects (such as project size, facility type, etc.). There are CRM solutions that are available as stand-alone or networked applications (e.g., Act!, GoldMine, Saleslogix), and there also CRM solutions that are available as subscription-based services over the Internet (e.g., Oracle, Siebel, Salesforce.com). Even Microsoft now offers a CRM package that integrates with its popular Outlook software.

If you're thinking of building your own system using Microsoft Access, FileMaker, or another off-the-shelf database system, bear in mind that the cost of building a system may actually be greater than the cost of buying a system, when you consider staff time, bug fixing, and so on. Many firms that build their own systems eventually migrate to one of the commercially available systems just cited. The advantages of an off-the-shelf system are significant: more features, better integration with other systems, and access to upgrades. One of the most important features that many off-the-shelf systems offer that most desktop-based homegrown systems lack is the capability to schedule future actions (for example, a reminder to call a potential client next Wednesday). Another benefit of commercially available systems is that several people can use the system to track their own leads; very often, homegrown systems can be used by only one person easily, usually a marketing coordinator.

In order to save costs, as mentioned, many firms just use a spreadsheet to track their leads. They create a simple database on a worksheet—with one lead per row, and fields across the columns to capture information about each lead.

Whether you're building a system, customizing a system, or created a worksheet to track leads, plan your fields carefully. For each lead you track, you may want to capture information such as the following:

- Client organization name
- Project name
- Opportunity stage (lead, prospect, short-listed, won/lost)
- Project size
- Project location
- Market (as defined by your firm; client industry or project type)
- Facility type
- Service (what you propose to do: architecture, interiors, planning, etc.)
- Estimated fee
- Key client contact
- Other contacts
- Your team
- Notes
- Next steps

Many firms structure the lead-tracking process around weekly business development reports and meetings. The meeting provides an incentive for key business developers to update their information on the reports, and provides a forum for discussing important leads and issues related to business development.

People: Your Clients and Other Contacts

If you purchase lead-tracking software, you'll probably be able to use it to store your mailing list/Rolodex as well. It's critical that you have an effective system for collecting, updating, and sharing contact information on your clients and other people that you deal with.

All of the lead-tracking/client relationship management software mentioned will enable you to track your contacts, but some programs include more robust list management/mass mailing/email capability than others. Make sure that you select contact management software that enables you to do all the things that you want with this information. If you're planning to create an email or printed client newsletter, you need your contact management software to help you to create and manipulate mailing lists.

If you don't plan to purchase or license relationship management software, you can use spreadsheet software, an electronic address book (such as Microsoft Outlook), or a database (such as Microsoft Access or FileMaker) to manage your contacts. If you follow this course, however, you may find that it's harder to share information (only one person can open an address book file at a time) and that it takes considerably more effort to prepare and utilize mailing lists.

Many firms have the challenge of integrating multiple contact management systems into one. Each partner or principal wants to maintain his or her own address book in Microsoft Outlook or some similar system. When it comes time to do a mailing, all of the different address books have to be integrated and sorted to prepare the mailing. Therefore, a much better choice is a scalable, integrated contact management system that everyone can use from the start. Ideally, you want to avoid maintaining duplicate information in more than one system, if at all possible.

Projects: Past Experience

When you're pursuing a new project, you need to identify what you've done in the past that's relevant to it, and you need to prepare qualifications to represent this relevant experience. If you're a small firm or a new firm without a significant portfolio, this will be a somewhat easier task than if you're a large firm or a firm with a long history. But eventually you'll need to institute some sort of system for tracking project information.

You have a few choices for how to track information on your projects: use an off-the-shelf system created for our industry (such as those available from Deltek or Cosential), create your own database system, or use a file system that is key-worded for attributes that you may want to search later.

The file system is the simplest to start, and if you set it up right, you can easily convert it to a database later. Create a form in a word processor (such as Microsoft Word) for information on your projects, fill out the form for each project (one file per project), and store all the files in the same folder. Make the form using a two-column table, with questions/categories down the left (project size, facility type, etc.) and answers on the right side. Then, when you want to find projects that are relevant to a current opportunity, you can use your computer's search feature to look for any files in the folder that contain certain text (such as "laboratory" or "Rhode Island") to find the appropriate projects.

Whether you're setting up a form for project information or creating a database, think about your fields carefully. Consider all the information that you might want to track about your projects, but don't make it overly complicated. Here are some fields that you may want to use:

- ▶ Client organization name
- ▶ Project name
- ▶ Project start date
- ▶ Completion date
- ▶ Project size
- ▶ Facility type (select all that apply from a list)
- ▶ Project location
- ▶ Construction cost
- ▶ Service(s) provided
- ▶ Project manager
- ▶ Project team
- ▶ Consultants
- ▶ Contractor
- ▶ Client contact
- ▶ Photographs available (yes/no)
- ▶ Project description

This is only an example. Feel free to customize and add to these fields to make your database or form fit your business.

One of the greatest challenges to collecting project information is determining when to collect it and who should collect it. Very often, a marketing coordinator who is not directly involved in the project is entrusted with the responsibility to gather project information. The marketing coordinator then has to track down this information from the project team. As this is usually a secondary responsibility of the marketing coordinator, the information doesn't get collected consistently; often, this information is updated only when it is required for a proposal. It would be far better to create a system wherein the project manager could provide and update project information throughout the development of the project.

Project information is more than just data, however. You'll want to capture images, plans, and other assorted files for use in marketing later. As you work on a project, be conscientious about the materials you gather and utilize, and organize them in a logical way that enables you to find them later. Everything that you create as part of the project process might be useful later in trying to win the next project. Store your site photos, your "before" photos, your renderings, your sketches, your construction snapshots, and your team photos in one place.

When the project is finished and you take snapshots or professional photographs, store those with other project documents in a physical project file, as well as in an electronic project file. Maintain both in order to easily accommodate information in the format in which it originally exists (you shouldn't have to scan hard copies or print electronic files to put them where they need to go).

Staff: Resumés and Statistics on Your Staff

Like project information, you need information on your staff when you're pursuing a project. You may need to know which architects are registered in a certain state, or speak a certain language, or have worked on laboratory projects. Resumés, of course, are the primary place where this information exists. In some cases, however, you may want to create or utilize a database for tracking information on your staff.

REMINDER

Your staff members are your most important resource. It's important to know what you have!

Think of your resumés as searchable files, like your project information forms. Organize them with every bit of information about your staff that you may want to know later. Consider adding an extra hidden page to your resumé files, on which to include important information that you want to capture but wouldn't necessarily show to clients or prospective clients. Put fields such as these in a table on this hidden page:

- Year joined your firm
- Year began practicing architecture
- Languages spoken
- States registered in
- Experienced in these project types
- Worked in these countries
- Usual project responsibility (project manager, architect, designer, etc.)

Depending on how large your staff is, you may want to consider using a database to track staff information. Both Deltek and Cosential have portions of their software packages designed to track staff information. If you build a project information database, it probably makes sense to add staff information to this database, so that you can track who worked on which projects.

Internal Communications

Getting the Message to Your Staff

14

In a firm that provides professional services, your people are your product and the basis for your brand. They're also your principal means of communicating with your clients and prospective clients. Your staff communicates with your clients through their actions, by delivering results that reinforce the image that your clients have about your firm. Your staff also communicates directly and verbally, telling your clients about your firm and what it can do to help them. In order to present a consistent image and message to your clients, you need to make sure that your staff understands what your firm is about and what their role is in the client communication process.

Many companies do a poor job communicating with their employees. The result of poor communications is often poor morale. If your staff doesn't understand or agree with your firm's direction, they won't feel good about working for your company. How you communicate sets the tone for the internal environment in your firm—your culture. Many services firms strive to create a "marketing culture," with each staff member connected to the firm's marketing efforts and aware of his or her role in the

TIP

Your staff is the first audience for your message; before you can sell your clients, you have to sell your employees.

TIP

Focus your message. If it's scattered, or changes frequently, it's going to be tough for your staff to follow.

process. In order to create a consistent culture, you need to promote good communications.

One attribute that most successful companies in any industry share is the ability to inspire their employees to believe in the company and commit to its mission. Your internal communications are critical to getting your staff to understand and accept your firm's identity, mission, and goals. If you can get your staff to understand and believe in your message, they'll spread it to your clients. If your staff is inspired and committed, they'll become truly persuasive spokespeople.

The Message: What Are You Trying to Say?

Before you can communicate with your staff, you have to decide what you want to say. What does your firm stand for? What do you need your staff to know about your firm? Do you have a important timely message for your staff, your clients, and the public? Is there a message you're trying to get out right now?

Whatever you're trying to say, recognize there is a difference between the external message and an internal message. The messages may be two sides of the same idea. If you're interested in promoting the idea of quality to clients, your internal message may be about why quality is important and what each employee's role is in assuring quality.

Let's consider a few messages that an architectural firm might want to promote, and how these messages can be echoed and reinforced by internal communications:

External Message	Internal Communication
We care about sustainability.	Each employee needs to learn about green design.
We're entering a new market.	Why we think we can succeed in this new market. How we're positioned in this market.
Our leadership is changing.	Who sets the direction of the firm? The values behind promotion.
We listen to our clients.	How we relate to clients. The importance of listening.
We care about people.	We care about you. We care about our clients.

You need to deliberately consider your message and plan how to promote it to each of your audiences. Your staff is the most important audience you have, and the first audience you need to consider in spreading a message.

The Medium: How Are You Going to Say It?

The most effective way you communicate with your staff is by example. Actions speak much louder than words. We each help to create our firm's culture through our actions and the tone that we set. If you want your staff to treat your clients attentively and with respect, first you have to treat your clients (and your staff) this way, and your staff will follow your example. Good behavior is contagious.

Beyond your behavior, you communicate through everything you say and write. Whether you're talking or writing to one person or your entire staff, everything you say influences how people feel and what they think about you and the firm. Choose your words carefully. You can communicate with your staff verbally, through print (policies, newsletters, memos, posters), and through email. Here are a few notes on each communication medium:

> *Verbal.* It's important for firm leadership to address the entire firm periodically. Sensitive news is best delivered face to face, but office meetings are also great for less critical communications. Schedule a monthly office meeting just to share news, give announcements, and celebrate recent successes.

> *Policies.* Create and distribute basic policy documents that are unique to your firm, such as a mission and values statement and a code of ethics. This gives employees a basic guideline for what is expected of them when they work for your firm.

> *Newsletters.* Periodic employee newsletters let everybody know what's going on in the firm. Include information on new projects, personal information/news on employees, announcements of new procedures or technology, and discussion of issues that are affecting your practice.

> *Memos.* When your firm has decided to make some kind of change, or when there's an important announcement, you may want to issue a memo, directly from the firm's leadership to the staff. When there is sensitive news (layoffs, organizational changes, etc.), be sure to release the memo as soon as possible to stifle the rumor mill.

- *Posters.* Posters are great for announcing upcoming events and important firm initiatives. They provide a persistent reminder in a prominent place. Posters are great for communicating simple, upbeat ideas.

- *Email.* A global email, sent to all employees, can take the place of a print memo or newsletter. Depending on the culture of your organization, you may want to use email to communicate news and important information. Remember that sensitive information is always best delivered in person, but when news breaks, you may want to send out an email to reach the staff immediately.

No matter which medium you select to deliver your message, it's critical that it be received as authentic and sincere. The fact that your message is heartfelt is actually more important than the medium by which it is delivered, so make sure that your emails and memos truly convey how important your message is to you.

Communication Tips: Getting the Message to Your Staff

Here are a few general tips about communicating with your staff:

- *Communicate your policies openly.* Create a mission and values statement, a code of ethics, benefits statements, and other standard policies. Make these easily accessible to your staff, so that everyone knows what is expected of them.

- *Regularly schedule communication.* Create regular forums for communication, whether these are staff meetings, newsletters, emails, or other forums.

- *Communicate often and easily.* Be comfortable communicating outside of the forums that you've created. When something is on your mind, get the word out.
- *Be clear.* Leave no room for ambiguity. If you want your staff to do something, tell them. Don't assume that they already know or that they can figure it out on their own.
- *Invite response.* When you're communicating with your staff, always ask what they think. In an email, encourage them to contact you if they have any ideas. When you speak, ask if your audience agrees with what you're saying. Listen carefully to any responses that you get, and adjust course if necessary.
- *Walk the talk.* Keep it real, and live up to your own hype. If your firm wants to be seen as one that cares about people, you have to care about people. If you truly believe in quality, what steps are you taking to promote quality? What about the environment? What have you done today to promote sustainable design?

Most important, you have to believe in your staff. Whatever your specific message about an issue or a policy, one message that you always need to promote to your staff is, "I trust you and respect you." If your staff doesn't believe in their own importance to you and the firm (or doesn't believe that you know how important they are), they probably won't listen to anything else you say, except to think about how your messages affect them personally. In a services firm, your people are everything; you have to respect them, trust them, and communicate effectively with them in order to become the organization that you want to be.

Client Communications

Newsletters, Web Sites, Direct Mail, Advertising, and Events

Though your staff is an incredibly powerful means of communicating with your clients, there are times when you want to reach out to your clients directly to promote your message. There are many choices for how to do this: You can communicate with your clients through client newsletters, your Web site, direct mail, advertising, even periodic client events.

Your message will be received differently based on which medium you use to deliver it. The most compelling way to deliver your message is to have it come from somebody else, either through a third-party endorsement or an article in the press (more on this in Chapter 16, "Media Relations and Awards"). The next most effective way to deliver your message is through your actions, by having your staff fulfill their promises to your clients and live up to the values that your firm espouses.

Beyond a third-party endorsement or what people can see about you through your actions, your communications enter into the realm of "spin." In today's media-saturated world, we're all suspicious of what people and companies say about themselves. How do you know when you can trust the message and when it's just hype?

TIP

There's nothing more compelling than a third-party endorsement from a satisfied client or a person in a position of authority.

No matter what form it takes, if the message is coming directly from you, it's going to be difficult to use it to convince anybody of anything. You can't just say "We care about the environment" and expect anyone to believe you. You have to back it up with facts. Where's the evidence? What have you done for the environment lately?

Even if you can't expect to win hearts and minds through your newsletter or Web site, there's still tremendous value in your client communications program. Your communications keep you in the client's mind. Your newsletter may not win you a project, but it will remind people that you exist, and reinforce what they already believe about you. If people feel that you're a creative firm, you can show them evidence to back it up. If people think you're an expert in one specific area, your communications give you a chance to prove it.

The Firm Web Site: Your Storefront on the Internet

Having a Web site is critical. Remarkably, some firms still don't have one, and regardless of the reason, it's a missed opportunity. A Web site enables you to promote a consistent image of your firm on the Internet. And because more and more people rely on the Web to do basic research, your site is a resource to potential clients, jobseekers, architecture students, possible partner firms, and others who are interested in architecture. Without a Web site, people may not be able to find you on the Internet; or if they do find you, they may only find information about you through third-party articles. These may say nice things about you and your firm (or they may not!), but they aren't as easy to locate as your Web site, and they probably won't provide information about you in a clear and digestible format.

To test your firm's exposure on the Web, do a search on your firm's name using Google, Yahoo!, or another search engine. See what comes up. You may be surprised at what you find—or what you don't find.

Here are a few quick tips on creating your firm's Web site:

TIP

Even if you have a Web page with only a picture and your phone number on it, that will at least give people a means by which to locate you on the Web and contact you for more information.

▶ *Don't obsess over graphics.* Just make the information clear. Don't worry about making the site incredibly elaborate or heart-stoppingly beautiful. Just try to convey who you are, what you're all about, and some of the work that you've done. Whatever you do, make your graphics look like they came from your firm. Strive for graphic consistency with your identity and your marketing materials.

▶ *Give the basic facts: who, when, where, what.* People visit Web sites looking for basic information. Who are you? When did your firm begin its practice? Where are you located? What kinds of projects do you do? You don't need to post a tremendous amount of information, but you do need to make the basics readily available. Include brief bios and photos of your key people. (Remember, in a services business, your people are both your product and your brand.)

▶ *Keep the content current.* Provide some areas for content on your home page that you can change every week or so. Perhaps provide links to current news articles on your firm or about recent projects. Whenever people check back, try to provide something new for them to look at.

- *Make your contact information easy to find.* Probably the most frequent complaint about corporate Web sites is that it's difficult to find a phone number. Make it easy for people to find out where you are and how to get in touch with you.

- *Hire a Web design consultant.* Don't try to design your Web site in-house. Even if you have some expertise in Web site development (which most architects do not), you need a third-party perspective on your firm and its image. What you want to say about yourself needs to be mediated and edited by someone with experience. Get some help, and your product will be much better.

Client Newsletters: What's the Latest?

Client newsletters are a great opportunity to let your clients know what's going on with your firm and to reinforce your key areas of expertise. Many firms miss this opportunity, either because they don't do newsletters at all, don't do them regularly, or don't do them well. A client newsletter is not a summary of your recent projects; it's a chance to speak to your clients and to provide them with insight and information that may be valuable to them.

Too many firms issue client newsletters that are mainly lists and blurbs on current and recent projects, with little context to tie the projects back to the concerns of their readers. Do your clients really care about the 20 other projects in addition to theirs that you're working on? They do if this information can help them, if those other projects provide some insight that means something to them. If it's just a list of projects, however, it won't mean anything.

Use your client newsletter to say something, express some insight, reveal some trends that mean something to your clients. Demonstrate that you're the expert in a specific area through your intelligence. What do your current projects have to say about what's going on in real estate, in design, in building trends? What's changing in your markets? Be interesting and informative to your audience. Take a position on the work in your markets, and be an advocate for change. What should we be doing differently? What could we be doing better?

The best client newsletters are personal and smart. They include a letter or statement from the leader or leaders of the firm. They include insight, as well as information on current projects. They speak to their audience. They demonstrate expertise. They are part white paper, part portfolio, part personal note, and part news report. The best newsletters are readable, clear, and focused on the client's issues.

Direct Mail: Flyers and Postcards

Some firms swear by direct mail. Other firms rarely use it. Direct mail usually takes the form of an announcement card or flyer relaying to your contacts and clients when something has happened: a name or address change, a new project, a new partner, some new award.

At their best, direct mail teaches the recipient something new about your firm. "Wow, I didn't know they did that kind of project." At the very least, direct mail keeps your name in mind. Even if, for an instant, the recipient just glances at the card or flyer before throwing it away, the card or flyer reinforces

TIP

Don't use your client newsletter just to talk about your projects. Say something. Take a position on an issue. Reveal an important trend.

your name in the recipient's mind, along with any other message that he or she happens to get before it hits the trash bin.

It's not enough to just stick a project photograph on the back of a postcard and call it direct mail. The photograph and the project have to carry some bit of news with them. Did the project just win an award? Is this a project that is transforming an underutilized area of town? Just as with your newsletter, it isn't enough that it's your project (who cares?); the question is, what does it mean to your audience?

When you develop a piece of direct mail, strive to create something about the card or flyer that makes people want to keep or to pass it along. If even some members of your audience tack up your card or flyer above their desks, you've managed to stake out valuable real estate in their hearts and minds.

TIP

Direct mail can be very helpful at getting the word out when you're trying to break into a new market.

One circumstance in which direct mail is very effective is when you're trying to break into a new market. Let's say you're trying to break into healthcare. If you've completed one or two healthcare projects, you can create a card or flyer that features these projects and send it out to people who may not have known that you work in this market. Voila! Your healthcare design practice is launched! The phone may not start ringing off the hook, but your direct mail campaign will help to get your name out there among your targets in this new market.

Holiday Cards: Saying That You Care

Holiday cards are a great once-a-year opportunity to show your clients that you care about them, that you've got them in mind. A generic card, no matter

Client Communications

how cute, doesn't say this as well as a card that you've carefully thought out and customized so that it could only come from you and your firm.

The best cards use humor and are highly personal. Cards that show a wreath or a tree miss an opportunity. Cards that show one of your projects (even if covered with snow) seem self-serving. Often the best and most memorable holiday cards show a firm's staff members engaged in some holiday activity.

Start thinking about your holiday card early, in late summer or early autumn. It takes time to design a good card. If you wait until Thanksgiving to think about it, you'll end up with another generic—and forgettable—holiday card.

TIP

Plan your holiday card early, to give you adequate time to come up with a personal message that could only have come from your firm.

Advertising: Reinforcing Your Position

Most architectural firms don't advertise very much. It isn't that they don't want to; it's that it's usually expensive, and the value of an architectural ad is tough to determine. Advertising doesn't teach anyone anything. It won't change anybody's perception about your firm or win you a project. So what good is it?

Advertising doesn't increase market share, it's true, but it helps to sustain it. Ads keep your firm in mind and reinforce your position. For this reason, advertising makes the most sense for the market leader, for the firm that is on top, to use to stake out their territory, shore up their defenses against the competition, and reaffirm their position.

Even though advertising makes sense for architectural firms only when the campaign is part of a larger strategy, those in the industry are often pres-

sured by trade publications to advertise. They propagate the myth that advertising will somehow miraculously help you grow your business, when in fact, most people are so oversaturated with ads that they don't pay attention to them at all anymore. Even if the people in your audience do see it, it probably won't register unless they know who you are already. As an architect, you're trying to reach a very small segment of the population: people who are potential clients for your services. Advertising is a shotgun medium; your odds of hitting one of your targets are slim. Your odds of hitting your target and motivating the client to give you a job are one in a million. One special kind of advertising is in event journals. Most annual fundraising banquets solicit contributions and offer contributors the opportunity to advertise in a journal that is given to every attendee. These ads are often used to congratulate the event's honoree. "XYZ firm congratulates Jim Smith, for his untiring dedication to the Juvenile Cancer and Diabetes Foundation." Usually the honoree is a prominent individual in the industry, so ads like this are primarily targeted to impress that individual. Be clear about your reasons for placing the ad, and create an ad that supports your strategy.

Trade Shows: Reaching Clients Where They Congregate

There are quite a few industry-related trade shows that architects attend. There are retail shows, airport shows, laboratory shows, shows for law firms, and others. The right show can be a great opportunity to meet prospective clients in a target industry.

To make the trade show experience rewarding, however, can take a significant investment of time and money. True, you can just show up at the show and mingle, but for maximum impact you'll probably want to have a booth at the show. And, if possible, you'll also want to host a session or have one of your staff be a speaker.

Think carefully about which shows you participate in and how much you invest in each show. You'll probably want to attend only those shows whose focus includes areas of your significant expertise. If you aren't a bona fide expert, you may not be comfortable at a trade show in a convention center filled with experts. But if you are an expert, a trade show is a great opportunity to show your stuff.

Remember why people are at the show: to learn, to have fun, to see people they know. They probably aren't specifically shopping for an architect (though some may be). When you attend the trade show, keep it loose and try to meet as many people as you can and have a good time. You may not win projects right away, but you can dramatically increase your network.

TIP

Creating and staffing a booth at a trade show can be an expensive undertaking. Target those trade shows that are most important to your marketing plan, and plan your participation in the trade show for maximum effect.

Special Events: Bringing Your Clients Closer and Treating Them Right

A great way to reach out to clients is not through the media at all, but through events. There are two main types of client events that you might host: *social* and *informative*.

Social events include holiday parties, art shows, and award dinners; that is, anytime you invite a group of clients to a social event for the purpose of building your personal relationship with them. Many marketers around the United States have found social events to be highly effective at building long-term relationships with clients. Architectural firms commonly host art shows in their offices, where they display the work of local artists. The opening-night cocktail parties are sometimes a favorite of clients. Other firms host dazzling holiday parties or summer picnics, and invite clients from all over to come and let their hair down.

To make an even greater impact on your clients and targets, create an informative event that provides your audience with some truly useful information, and they'll show up, they'll remember you, and you'll be able to strengthen your personal and work bonds. If you're trying to reach healthcare professionals, host a roundtable on the future of healthcare design. Roundtables and other knowledge-sharing events can position your firm as the expert in a given field. If you get some key figures in the field to show up, you may have to turn people away. And you may even be able to get members of the press to cover the event (see Chapter 16).

The lesson: Knowledge is, in fact, power. And people want it. Knowledge is even more important than dinner or cocktails. Provide your clients with knowledge that can help their careers, and they'll remember you.

TIP

When a party isn't enough, create an event that provides clients with useful information or other professional benefit.

Media Relations and Awards

Communicating with the Press

16

Many people use the term *public relations* (PR) to refer to the communications activities they engage in to relate to everyone outside of the firm who is not a client or a prospective client. This chapter is about a specific slice of public relations: media relations and awards. Generally speaking, public relations isn't relevant to most architectural firms; the public, in fact, doesn't even know you exist. How much of a relationship do you really have with the general public? If you're like most firms, you'd probably love just to get mentioned or to have an article about one of your projects published in a magazine or a newspaper.

Public relations is an issue for famous people: for heads of state, for movie stars, for star architects. Public relations is about how people who have a public relate to it. Do you have a public? No? Then you need *media relations*, to get your projects in the press so that, eventually, you gain a public.

Media Relations: Getting Your Name in the Papers

Like many architects, you would probably consider sacrificing a client to an ancient Sumerian god if

REMINDER

When most people say "public relations" they mean "media relations."

doing so would get your firm mentioned in the newspaper. (It would, by the way, but not in the section you'd like. And you'd have to make sure that you pitched the story in just the right way. . . .)

You want to get your firm's name, its stories, its pictures in newspapers, magazines, and on television? It's easy. There are only two steps:

1. Do something newsworthy.
2. Figure out why it's newsworthy and convince the media of that fact.

Step 2 is much harder, which is why the media relations industry exists. It isn't enough just to do something remarkable, because most people probably won't recognize it as such. You have to be able to demonstrate to the media that it's remarkable and explain why. You have to sell it.

Seriously, a lot is involved in this simple two-step process. There's strategy. There's identifying stories, then recasting, prioritizing, and promoting them to carefully targeted media outlets. All of this is vitally important to getting coverage in the media for your firm and your projects.

Sometimes it's easy and sometimes it's extremely difficult to get media coverage. If you're working on a truly important project, you'll have a hard time keeping it out of the papers. With the reconstruction of Lower Manhattan following the terrorist attacks of September 11, 2001, for example, the firms involved have employed media relations professionals *not* to get them press coverage, but to manage what gets in the press. In contrast, if you're working on a relatively nondescript academic building, it may be tough to get any coverage at all—unless you can find an angle and pitch a story.

Publications are, in fact, looking for stories all the time. How do you decide what your story is and which media outlet(s) you want to pitch it to?

Media Strategy and Planning: Making a Plan to Get the Coverage You Want

TIP

Be realistic. It's going to be a lot easier to get press for an important project than for an unremarkable one.

Creating a media strategy is a process of matching up the publications in which you'd like to be featured or mentioned with the stories that you have. A shotgun approach is not particularly effective with the media—it isn't enough to have a somewhat interesting story and to send a press release everywhere and hope that someone recognizes the value of the story. You need to carefully target publications and other media outlets and prepare your stories for those outlets specifically.

Developing your media strategy combines self-assessment (What's interesting about us? What have we done lately that people will want to hear about?) with an understanding of how the media works, what media outlets are out there, and what they're looking for. To make it simple, let's group the media into three tiers: broad business/entertainment media, trade publications, and architectural press.

> ➤ *Broad business/entertainment media.* This comprises almost everything: *The New York Times, Entertainment Weekly, People Magazine,* CNN, your local paper. There are thousands upon thousands of publications, news programs, radio shows, and Web sites that you may be able to convince to do a story on your firm or some of your work. The challenge here is in choosing which publications and other media outlets to

target, and in developing stories aimed for those.

▶ *Trade publications*. These are what your clients read, publications such as *Laboratory Facility Week*, *Health Care Today*, and *Data Center World*. These are fictional names, but there are thousands of professional publications like these, with extremely focused and specialized circulations. Depending on your work and your expertise, it can be relatively easy to get a project covered or even to byline an article in a trade publication. Become familiar with the publications that your clients read. If you want to be perceived as an expert in a specific field, get published in a trade publication.

▶ *Architectural press*. These are the publications your competitors read—*Architectural Record, Architectural Digest, Architecture Magazine, Interior Design, Architectural Review*. Many architects drool at the possibility of having their projects featured in these publications. Having a project covered in *Architectural Record* says to the architect, "I've arrived. I'm taken seriously as a professional. My work is important." But it can be good for more than stoking an architect's ego; it can also be advantageous for recruiting purposes and to serve as a clipping or reprint material to include with a qualifications package or to mail out to clients and prospective clients. (Reprints cost a bundle, however, so be prepared to pay a few thousand dollars for the right to reproduce the article and the cost of printing.) What these publications will not generally do is enable you to get in front of your clients and prospective clients, unless your clients are architects or true fans of architecture.

Make a list of the publications you'd like to reach and study them carefully. Read them dutifully. Learn what kinds of stories they publish. Look for opportunities to meet the editors, at industry events or other public forums.

Make another list of the stories that you have to tell. These can be newsworthy projects or interesting facts or events in the development of your firm. Anything that will be interesting to your list of target publications is fair game: One firm that was very interested in sustainable design was featured in the press because of the compost pile that they placed on the roof of their office. Ownership and leadership transition are always interesting topics, as is the foundation of a new firm.

Your list of stories can't just be an enumeration of your recent and current projects. Projects, by themselves, are not necessarily newsworthy. What's the story? What's the verb? "Our firm was hired to renovate . . ." Who cares? Is your project the first of its kind in some way? Is it the largest of something? Does it signal some kind of sea change for a town, a downtown area, a corporation, a university? What's new and different about it? What makes it special?

The fact that your project is reaching an important milestone (groundbreaking, topping out, completing construction, and so on) is an excuse to place a story, but it isn't the story. Buildings are built all the time. Every groundbreaking, every topping out, is not reported by the press. The story is made timely by the event, but this isn't what makes it news. It's news because it's an important project.

Once you've got a list of publications and a list of stories, try to match them up. Figure out which publications might be interested in which stories. One

AT HAND

Developing a media strategy involves identifying target publications and the stories that you have to tell, and making a plan for which stories to promote to which publications.

architectural firm had just completed a big project that happened to be the largest concrete building in the state. Maybe this fact wouldn't be much help in getting the firm written up in *The New York Times* or the *San Francisco Chronicle*, but you can bet that *Concrete Week* was all over it.

Talking to the Media: Getting Your Story Out There

So you know which publications you're trying to reach and which stories you'd like to place in these publications. How do you tell them your stories? Do you write a press release and send it out, far and wide? Do you call an editor on the phone? Do you send an email?

Knowing the editor can be very helpful. If you know the editor, you'll know how to position the story and how to make contact. Does the editor prefer email, voice mail, or a letter? Beyond that, if the editor knows you, he or she will be much more likely to listen to your story and to take you seriously.

How you pitch the story to an editor will depend on the story, the editor, and your relationship. Here are a few basic tips:

> ▶ *Find your angle.* What's the story? Why will this editor care?

> ▶ *Know the publication.* Make sure this story is appropriate to this publication.

> ▶ *Be personal.* Don't send a general press release. Send a customized email to one editor, or leave a voice mail. Be polite, and be human.

> ▶ *Be concise.* Be able to define the story in one sentence. Don't waste the editor's time.

> ➤ *Don't be a pest.* A few days after you send the email or leave the message, try to make contact again. If you can't get through, let it go and move on.

Editors and reporters are part of your network just like clients, contractors, and consultants. They're good people to know, and it's important to build relationships with them. They can provide insight into their publications and the broader media world. But in order to network with them effectively, the relationship has be reciprocal—you have to help them out, too. Is there a way that you can be a source for reporters and editors? Try to build a relationship with an editor whereby you call him or her when you've got a story, and he or she calls you in pursuit of one.

Awards Submissions: The Long Road Is Sometimes the Most Satisfying

A great way to get a project published is to win a design award. Many awards are either hosted by design publications or by organizations that have a relationship with a magazine whereby the winners are published. Design awards can be very tough to win; in fact, the award entry itself can be quite a rigorous process. Moreover, it can be expensive: There are often entry fees of several hundred dollars to submit your project for consideration.

When you're considering submitting your project for an award, become familiar with the purpose and history of the award. Which projects won last year? What kinds of projects win? What's the criteria?

Who's on the jury? What kinds of work do they do? What are their tastes?

There's no point wasting your time and money if you don't have a chance to win. Be objective. Look at your project. Is this project worthy of this award? Do you meet all the criteria? Is your photography good enough? If you were a judge, would you select this project?

Winning an award can be incredibly gratifying, as well as a real boost to your business development efforts and staff morale. One firm designed a high-profile retail project that just kept winning awards. It won the coveted *BusinessWeek/Architectural Record* award. It was *Chain Store Age* magazine's Store of the Year. It even received a Clio award from the advertising industry. The lesson here is that when it happens, it happens. The right project at the right time in the right place will win almost automatically. It's very difficult to plan it. Sometimes you get lucky. Just be ready when the time comes to submit the entry.

TIP

Don't waste your time or money on competitions you can't win. Familiarize yourself with the awards program and see what types of projects win. Make an objective assessment: Do you really have a chance?

Media Relations Tips: How to Make It Easier on Yourself

Media relations is a profession unto itself. Many books and articles have been written on working with the media. It's a frequent topic of local Society for Marketing Professional Services (SMPS) events around the country. This chapter has only scratched the surface. If media relations is a specific focus for you, seek out additional resources.

To close, here are a few tips on creating and sustaining a successful media relations program:

- *Ask permission.* Get your client's permission before starting to promote a project. Believe it or not, the client may not want to have the project reported in the press for one reason or another. Respect your client's wishes.

- *If you can, partner with your client.* Very often, your clients will have more resources and deeper pockets than you. If the client wants to promote the project to the media, you can work with the client's media relations people or consultants to get the project in the press. It doesn't hurt to ask, and it can save you a lot of effort and money to collaborate with your client.

- *Don't waste your time.* Not all stories are interesting and not all projects are publishable. Don't bang your head against the wall. Pick the best stories you've got and push those. You won't be successful with everything. Just keep moving.

- *Make friends with the editors.* If they know you, they can help you. If you know them, you'll know what they're interested in and the angles they respond to.

- *See it from the editor's point of view.* Always ask, "Why is this interesting? Why should somebody care about this?" It's not enough that it's a project that is being built. What makes it news?

- *Get professional help.* Media relations is serious business, and it's tough to do it yourself. There are many fabulous consultants working in this industry who have built their careers on media and public relations. They already know the editors, and they know how to pitch a story.

Media relations is one area in which firms with dedicated staff and good consultants have a tremen-

TIP

Getting a good article in the press can have significant benefits. Clients have been known to read a favorable article and pick up the phone to call a firm.

dous advantage over those without. The best media and public relations consultants are expensive, and worth it.

The results can be truly significant. One good article in the right publication can actually have your phone ringing off the hook. The reputations of many star architects have been made in the media, not so much by their projects, but by how their projects (and their personalities) have been reported by the press. Some architects invest more effort and resources in media relations than they do in business development. What if, instead of having to compete for work, a client reading an article in a newspaper or magazine called you to hand you a project? It happens. Sow your seeds in the media, and they'll grow into projects.

Photography
Creating the Right Image

17

Photography can make a tremendous difference in how your work is perceived. High-quality photography makes your work look good; bad photography can make it look ill conceived or cheaply constructed. Obviously you want your photos to show your work in its best light. Unfortunately, it can be frustratingly difficult to evaluate your own portfolio objectively, because you know your projects inside and out and you've seen the same photos a thousand times. But would you think they look as good to somebody who has never seen them and doesn't know the project? If you can't be objective about your photographs, how can you be sure they present your projects as you want them to be seen?

To a great extent, the quality of your photographs is the result of the investment of time and money you make in the photography process. Good photos generally cost more than bad photos, and take longer to create. You can get a bad photo in 30 seconds: just point and click. A good photo can take hours to set up and shoot, and can be an expensive investment. Shooting a project can potentially cost up to $20,000, or even more, based on the photographer, the number

REMINDER

Good photos make your work look good. Bad photos can give a false impression.

TIP

Partner with contractors and consultants to reduce your firm's total investment in the photo shoot.

of shots and the time frame, whether the shoot is inside or outside, required expenses, and more.

Nevertheless, good photography is a prudent investment. Photos of your work can be used throughout your marketing program: on your Web site and in your brochure, presentations, publications, press releases, award submissions, direct mail, ads—almost anywhere. High-quality photos help convince your audience of your design capability and expertise. More than showing your work in its best light, exceptional photographs can actually have an emotional impact on the viewer.

In order to plan your photography program, you need to decide how much you're prepared to spend. Fortunately, not all the money has to come out of your pocket. Hopefully, you can share the expense with the rest of the team—the contractor, the engineer, vendors and suppliers, other consultants who worked on the project, and even the client may want photos for their marketing materials and personal use. If you can get a group to share the cost of the photo shoot, your costs will go down dramatically. Instead of spending $10,000 to shoot a project, for example, you can split it 10 ways and spend much less, or shoot 10 times as many projects.

Unless your firm does very few projects, you probably can't shoot every one; it's just too time-consuming and cost-prohibitive. You have to be selective, and deciding which projects to shoot involves assessing costs and benefits. Where will your photography money be best spent? Which projects absolutely have to be photographed? Which are optional? When considering photographing a project, ask yourself these questions:

- What's remarkable about this project?
- Is this project unique in your portfolio?
- Do you think this is a "publishable" project?
- What uses do you anticipate for the photos?
- Will the client give permission to shoot the project?
- Will other project participants split the cost of the shoot?

Prioritize your projects based on how important they are to your portfolio, how much mileage you think you can get out of them, and how much support you have from the client and other project participants. In some cases, of course, you may need to go it alone, and shoot a project that is important to your firm without much support from other team members.

Make a photography plan and budget on a semi-annual or quarterly basis. Looking at your photography as a program, rather than on a shoot-by-shoot basis can help you to optimize your investment by hiring a single photographer for multiple projects or approaching one contractor or consultant to contribute to several shoots. A periodic photography plan and budget can also help bring some control to what can be a chaotic (and expensive) process.

TIP

Look at your overall photography plan on a quarterly or semiannual basis to find ways to optimize your investment.

Planning a Shoot: Hiring a Photographer and Working Out the Details

The choice of a photographer should not be taken lightly. The selection of the photographer will have greater influence over the quality of your photography than any other factor. Good photographers can work miracles, and generally charge several thousand dollars a day for their time. It's going to be expensive anyway, so you might as well pick a photographer who you believe can give you the best results.

Don't take chances. Find a photographer who has proven experience with similar projects. Look in architectural magazines for projects that resemble yours in one way or another and, if you like what you see, track down the photographer. If you have a friend who is an editor or a reporter, ask him or her for recommendations. Ask a friend at a firm that you respect. Try to always get a referral for any photographer you're considering

TIP

Don't hire a photographer without a referral.

When you find a photographer whose work you like and who has experience with similar projects, call and arrange to meet, to review his or her portfolio and to discuss the project. Your objective at this point is to try to determine whether the photographer is a good fit for you and your firm, and right for this project. When you talk about the project, listen carefully to what the photographer advises in terms of film format (positive/negative film, size of film, perhaps digital), how and when to shoot the project, whether or not to use people in the shots, and so on; then consider whether you agree with what you heard. Keep in mind the photographer is more than just the person who will take the pictures; a good photographer also can be your consultant and advisor about how you visually represent the work of your firm. Leading architectural photographers know the editors at the major magazines and so can help ensure that your projects are presented in a way that is appropriate for your target publications.

If you like the photographer, and believe this person is a good fit for you and the project, it's time to talk about rates and terms. Most professional photographers retain the rights to their images, granting their client the right to use them for certain purposes. So it's important that you discuss how you want to use the images *before* retaining the photographer, and then get it in writing. Will you have the right to use the images in your publications, in magazines, on the Web? How long do you have the right to use the images? Do the client and participating consultants (if any) have the right to use the images? Can you make your own reproductions or does the photographer control the negatives? Under what circumstances must you credit the photographer? How? Have the photographer sign an agreement that grants you the license to use the photographs according to the terms that you both agree to. This eliminates any possible misunderstandings on either part later.

Once you've come to terms with the photographer, you can start to plan the shoot. When can the project be shot? (What works with the client's schedule, the photographer's schedule, and your schedule?) What time of day? How long will it take? Will the photographer need an assistant? What about lighting? Walk the project with the photographer and plan the shoot in detail. Using a site plan or floor plan, mark off each shot and discuss what will be required. Bring along a Polaroid or a digital camera to snap the pictures that you're considering as part of the shoot.

Make sure that the client is on board with the shoot; confirm it in writing, in the form of a permission agreement that allows you to shoot the project on a certain date and to use the resulting images in specific ways. Make this agreement very explicit to avoid any misunderstandings.

 TIP

Make sure your agreement with the photographer is in writing, signed by both of you. Likewise, request the client to give you permission in writing, as well as any participants in the photo shoot. Written agreements protect you from misunderstandings later.

Communicate clearly with other firms that may be participating in the shoot. How many shots will they get? Of which views? How much will they be expected to pay? Co-sign a short agreement with them that spells out how many images they will get, for what uses, and specify their share of the cost. Collect money from the other participants *before* any pictures are taken.

Shooting the Project: Much More Than Point and Click

A photo shoot is, ideally, a collaboration between the designer of the project and the photographer. You have to do it together; you can't minimize or delegate your participation in the process. Questions come up on the spot, in the field, and decisions have to be made—about where to place people, whether a certain feature needs to be in the shot, and so on. As the designer of the project and the photographer's client, you have be there to provide input to these decisions. If you aren't there, the photographer will be forced to use his or her own judgment, and you may not agree with the results, so work collaboratively with the photographer throughout the shoot and stay until the very end.

When you're on the shoot, be prepared for how long it takes and how much work can be involved. It can literally take hours to set up a single shot. For an interior shot, you may have to rearrange furniture, clean off desks, scrub floors, set up lights. For an exterior shot, you may need people to move cars, wait until the light is right, and so on. It doesn't make sense to cut corners at this point: You're paying the photographer, you've gotten the client's

TIP

Don't cut corners when you're on the shoot. Do everything that you can to get the best possible shot.

Photography: Creating the Right Image

permission to be there to shoot, you might as well do it right. Make sure you get the shots you want, and don't let anything stand in your way. Consider carefully whether you want people in your shots. People provide context to an environment or a structure; they make a space seem lived in, provide a building with some sense of scale, and give the impression that the project actually exists somewhere on the planet Earth. On the downside, people can date the photo through the style of their hair and clothing. And if they look at all uncomfortable, awkward, or posed, they can ruin the photo. If you decide to have people in your shots, make sure that they are dressed appropriately and are prepared to stay for a while; and don't forget to have them sign a photo release that gives you permission to use their image in your marketing materials, on your Web site, and so on.

Depending on which camera technology the photographer is using, you may have the opportunity to see Polaroids between the full exposures. These rough shots can help you and the photographer to improve the framing or positioning of a shot. When the photographer shows you a Polaroid, study it carefully. Does it show what you had hoped? Is there anything that needs to be moved? Is the camera in the right spot? Is the angle right?

Trust the photographer. You selected this professional because of his or her experience and style and the belief that you could work well with this person. The shoot is not the time to question the photographer's recommendations, unless you feel that the shoot is not going well, that the images are not capturing the project. Let the photographer lead the process.

 TIP

When you're on the shoot, review the photographer's work to make sure that he or she is capturing the project as intended.

After the Shoot: Finishing and Using Your Photos

After the shoot, it may take the photographer a week or more to process the film and give you test prints. The process of reviewing and adjusting the prints can be arduous, and will require patience. The photographer can be an important advisor through this process. The photographer wants his or her work to look good, and will generally make an effort to make sure that you receive the best possible result.

Collaborate with the photographer on the prints, but let him or her manage the process of perfecting the images. Tell the photographer what you honestly think. Are you happy with the product? Do the images look like the project? Is the color off? Is it too light? Too dark? If so, the photographer or the photo lab can probably adjust the print to be closer to what you have in mind.

Sometimes you'll want to retouch the images, as well. Is there a fire hydrant in front of your building that you want to remove? An exit sign? The photographer can probably recommend a photo retoucher who can help, and can review the retoucher's work to make sure that you're getting the highest quality.

Once you're happy with the images, order copies of the photos in all of the different formats that you need. Order a set of prints for the client and sets for each consultant or contractor who has contributed to the shoot. Take orders from your staff for their portfolios. You'll save money by placing a larger order now, so consider getting a few spare prints. Do you need slides for any reason? Do you need transparencies?

TIP

Even after you have the prints in hand, there's still a lot that can be done to alter the exposures and retouch the images, if you feel it's necessary. Though doing so can be expensive, it may be worth it to correct a flawed image.

Unless the photographs were taken in a digital format, you'll need to scan your images for use in your marketing materials and on your Web site. The quality of your scans is critical to how good your images will look on the screen or when you print them. Ask the photographer for a recommendation for how to get the best possible result. Some photographers like to manage the process of scanning the images, and may even want to do it themselves.

Organize your physical and electronic image library so that the images are readily accessible and useful to you later. In your physical library, consider maintaining separate files for each format—one file for prints, one for slides, one for transparencies, each organized by project. In your electronic image library, establish standard sizes and formats for your images, based on final application. For example, you may want to have each image in three different resolutions: one for Web and on-screen (96 dpi), one for in-house prints (200 dpi), and one high-resolution for the press, making photographic-quality prints, and large-format applications. As your image library grows, you may want to consider building a keyword database for your images, so that you can type in a search ("stairs," for example) and see all the relevant images at once.

TIP

Organize your print and electronic image library so that you can readily find the images you're looking for, when you need them, in the formats you require.

Marketing Staff and Consultants

Who Can Help You?

18

Described at length throughout this book are many activities related to marketing an architectural firm. You don't have to do them alone. If you're really going to try to do even half of them, you're going to need help. Even if you're a sole practitioner, you should still consider bringing on a consultant part-time to help with some of these tasks.

The challenge is in determining what is reasonable for you and your firm to hope to accomplish and how much help you need to do it. At what point do you need to hire a full-time marketer to work with you? Do you need more than one? There is some rough correlation between size of firm and number of marketing staff. Generally, firms hire their first full-time marketer when they have 25 to 35 staff members, and their second when they have around 65 to 70. From there, the ratio of marketers to staff is about 1 to 50, or a little lower. It depends, of course, on how diverse your practice is, how effective your marketing is, and how hard you're pushing into new markets.

Firms follow different strategies for hiring marketers and building their marketing team, depending on their specific objectives and requirements. For

RULE OF THUMB

Most firms have around one marketer for every 50 employees (or a little less). Firms tend to consider hiring their first full-time marketer when they get to have 25 to 35 staff.

some firms, media relations are critical, and their first hire may be an in-house media relations director. Other firms may use a consultant for media relations, but start their marketing team with a marketing director and later add a coordinator.

If you're a sole practitioner, or work in a firm of fewer than 25 people, you'll need to be creative to figure out how to address your marketing needs. You could hire a marketing consultant to help, or you could find one employee—either an architect or an administrative staff member—to be a part-time marketer. In either case, you'll need to be very clear about the required tasks and your expectations in order to provide the necessary guidance for your part-time marketer.

TIP

If you don't have the resources to hire a full-time marketer, you'll need to be creative to address your firm's marketing needs. Hire a marketing consultant or identify a current staff member who can be a part-time marketer.

Marketing Staff: Who Are They?

As described in the introduction to this book, architectural marketing is a relatively new field, having a total history of about 30 years. The idea that architects would have professionals working for them to help them build relationships and bring in work is an even newer idea, consequently the profession of architectural marketing is still somewhat undefined and in the process of formation. Most architectural marketers grew into their roles from some other field. While most have college degrees, very few studied architecture or marketing; many are artists or writers or architectural historians. They tend to learn what they know about marketing on the job, by being mentored by other marketers, or by teaching themselves the hard way while working with an architectural firm. Successful architectural marketers share many attributes: They tend to be flexible, creative, smart, and have excellent interpersonal skills, both in terms of communication and their ability to collaborate.

Though there isn't much available in the way of formal education for architectural marketers, a rough career path has developed over time. It is increasingly common to find architectural firms that recognize their marketers as integral to their operations, and promote them within the firm's organizational or appointments structure. Many marketers are now associates or senior associates or associate partners; a few are principals. The following are the most common titles for architectural marketers and a brief description of what they do:

REMINDER

Unlike architects, most marketers do not have a professional degree in their chosen field. Most learned about marketing on the job, rather than in school.

Marketing Director

> ▸ Directs the marketing effort for the firm.

> ▸ Reports directly to firm principals.

> ▸ Leads the marketing team.

> ▸ Has responsibility for creating and implementing the marketing plan and marketing budget.

Marketing Coordinator

> ▸ Prepares proposals, presentations, awards submissions, and other marketing materials.

> ▸ Works with the firm's staff to gather data and create materials.

Media Relations Director

> ▸ Represents the firm to the media.

> ▸ Is responsible for creating and implementing the firm's media strategy.

> ▸ Maintains relationships with editors, reporters, and other representatives of the media.

Business Developer

> ▸ Makes contact with potential clients and sets up meetings for the firm's principals.

> ▶ May be an industry specialist, with established existing relationships in a given industry that can help open doors.

In larger firms, there are many variations on these themes. There may be marketing managers, graphic designers, archivists, and other roles created to fill the needs of the firm. For additional descriptions and more detailed information on the roles in marketing, a good resource is Sally Handley and Sharyn Yorio's book *Charting Your Career Path: Opportunities for Professional Service Marketers in the 21st Century* (The Society for Marketing Professional Services, 2001). A portion of this book is a summary of a survey that Handley and Yorio conducted on the "Current State of the Profession" of marketing professional services; it provides a detailed assessment of the status, training, and career of services marketers.

Handley and Yorio's book is published by the Society for Marketing Professional Services (SMPS), which has emerged as an important resource for marketers and principals in the fields of architecture, engineering, and construction. The SMPS provides training and other resources through its network of local chapters nationwide. Many marketers find membership and participation in the SMPS to be an essential part of their support network. And because there are, at most, only a few marketers in most firms, the SMPS can help provide connection and mentoring that many marketers can't get inside their firms.

Marketing for architects is a tough job. Burnout is a constant problem. In marketing, you're always under the gun, always working under a deadline, always pushing to get something out the door. It's not uncommon for marketers to work an average of 60 hours a week or more; there's always more to do, something else to take care of. As a result, many marketers leave the industry after a year or two, and less than half stay for more than five years. As an architect, it's important to recognize the challenges your marketers face and to support them. If you've got a good marketing staff, you won't want to have to replace them every year. Take care of them, help them to prioritize tasks, and make sure that they don't work too hard for too long. Everybody deserves a break, and if your marketers don't get it, they'll leave you.

TIP

If you want your marketer to stay with your firm, treat him or her well. No one is going to slave away indefinitely if they are undervalued.

Aside from the workload, another key factor that drives turnover is how good your firm is and how you are as a professional to work with. Marketers take responsibility for getting things done on time—proposals, presentations, qualifications, award submissions. Do you support this or do you frustrate it? When your marketer says he or she needs it Thursday, do you hand it in on Friday? When you receive an RFP or other important communication from a prospective client, do you give it to the marketer right away or do you hang onto it for a while? Does the marketer feel as if he or she knows what's going on, or that he or she only gets selected information? The marketer wants to be your partner in building the business of your firm. It's a collaborative process. If you aren't collaborating, your marketer is likely to go somewhere else.

Marketing Consultants: Calling in the Experts

Whether or not you have marketing staff, there are times when you may need to hire a consultant. Your marketing staff is your ongoing collaborator in building your business. Your staff may have certain expertise in one area or another, but you can't expect your marketing staff to be experts in everything. Sometimes you'll need to call in an expert consultant to help with a specific problem, exercise, or long-term initiative.

There are quite a few consultants out there who specialize in marketing-related areas and who are familiar with the business of architecture. Here are a few types of consultants that you may want to consider retaining:

> *Strategic marketing consultant.* Usually a marketer who now works for several firms on a variety of strategic tasks such as creating strategic and marketing plans, developing new materials, and so on.

> *Brand consultant.* You may want to work with a brand consultant if you're considering a name change or new graphic identity. Brand consultants help you to focus your thinking about who you are and who you want to be.

> *Business developer.* Rather than hire a business developer as a permanent employee, you may want to hire a business developer on a consultant basis. Usually a business development consultant will have a network of existing relationships in a given industry.

> *Freelance graphic designer.* Preparing a brochure or other publication and want it to look good? Hire a freelance graphic designer, and get a high-quality design without having to commit to a full-time position.

> *Web designer.* For the initial launch of your Web site or a significant update, you may want to retain a graphic designer who specializes in

interactive design. This is an entirely different discipline from designing for print, so make sure you hire a designer with a significant online portfolio.

➤ *Freelance writer.* Writing a monograph, an article, a brochure? Hire a freelance writer to craft your ideas into prose.

➤ *Media relations/public relations.* Media relations and public relations consultants are an enormous help to getting your stories and projects into the press. The advantage of hiring a consultant who works with other clients is that they likely know more editors and reporters than a permanent staff member might.

➤ *Photographer.* While a few larger firms may have an in-house photographer, the best talent works freelance. Hiring a freelance photographer lets you pick the right photographer for each assignment.

➤ *Videographer.* You may have occasion to shoot a video of your work or about your firm. You may be able to find a production team composed of a camera operator and an editor that can do everything that you need.

➤ *Presentation skills or sales training consultants.* Interested in improving your presentation skills or learning new sales techniques? There are many consultants out there who work in the industry and specialize in marketing skills development.

The relationship that you have with a consultant is very different from the relationship that you have with an employee or staff member. To the consultant, you are the client. There are real advantages to hiring a consultant to help you, rather than counting on permanent staff:

> *Get the right person for the right job.* If you're hiring a consultant for one assignment, you can find a specialist who has done it before and has the exact skills and experience that you need.

> *Less commitment.* You can take a risk with a consultant. If it doesn't work out, you can terminate the relationship easily. It's much more difficult to end a relationship with an employee.

> *More leverage.* Because you're paying the consultant on an assignment-by-assignment basis, the consultant is bound to deliver the work when he or she said. If you don't get the work, the consultant may not get paid.

> *Can try out different professionals.* If you like, you can use a different photographer for each photo shoot, or a different graphic designer for each brochure. You can learn the strengths of each, and keep trying them until you find the one you like the most.

When you retain a consultant, the pressure is on both of you to make the terms of your agreement clear. You need to communicate to the consultant what you expect him or her to deliver, and by when. The consultant needs you to understand how his or her compensation will be structured and when you will need to pay. It is in everybody's best interest to get the terms of this agreement in writing; perhaps the consultant can prepare a proposal for both of you to sign.

One of the most challenging aspects of retaining a consultant (in fact, in marketing as a whole; see the next chapter!) is determining whether you're getting

TIP

Get the terms of your relationship with the consultant in writing. Ask the consultant to submit a proposal for his or her services.

your money's worth. How much is quality worth? When is it worth it to hire the best consultants, and when can you make do with in-house talent? For most consulting services related to marketing (photography, public relations, marketing strategy, etc.) it's going to be very difficult to apply any sort of objective metrics to the activities of the consultant that justify the cost. What you can do, however, is apply a level of subjective evaluation. Here's how:

1. Figure out the total cost for a given activity (a photo shoot, getting an article in the newspaper, creating a Web site).
2. Find some basis for comparison. Ask a friend at another firm what they pay, or find some history on what similar activities have cost your firm.

Do you feel like you got your money's worth? If you feel good about the consultant, there's no need to look further. If you feel like you spent more than you should have, make a different plan of attack for next time—to use in-house talent or a less expensive consultant, or to negotiate a different rate or a flat fee.

Evaluating Your Performance
Is Your Marketing Working?

19

So, you spent about 7 percent of your total revenue on marketing last year. Was it worth it? Lots of proposals went out the door. You made a bunch of presentations. You won a few jobs. Was that money well spent, or would you have done as well if you had spent half as much? How can you tell?

It's very challenging to evaluate the success of your marketing efforts, so challenging, in fact, that many firms don't bother. What metrics do you apply to measure marketing? Do you look at increased revenue? Do you look at win rate? Do you look at market penetration?

Your marketing plan is the only yardstick that you can use to evaluate your marketing success. In order to determine whether you've been successful, you have to define success. What are your goals? Figure out what you want to accomplish, try to accomplish it, and then determine if you were successful.

In a survey conducted in early 2003, Sally Handley of The Marketing Partnership found that approximately 50 percent of professional service firms (architects, engineers, contractors, etc.) had no marketing plan. If you don't have a plan, how can you possibly evaluate whether you're successful?

REMINDER

Make a marketing plan and revise it every year. Without it, you have no way to guide your efforts and no way to evaluate whether what you're doing is working.

You haven't defined what success means, so how do you know if you've hit the mark?

Let's say you've written a marketing plan, and it says, "We want to have a 30 percent win rate on proposals submitted and we want to increase our revenue by 10 percent." These are metrics that are easy to measure. Everything that you do will be in service to these goals: selecting projects to pursue, submitting proposals, making presentations, getting mentioned in the press. Unless you apply this level of rigor to your marketing planning, you'll never really know whether your marketing efforts are working. As the aphorism goes, "If you don't know where you're going, you'll probably end up someplace else." Think of your marketing plan as your map. Without the map, you won't know where you're going and you won't know where you are once you arrive.

Without a plan, there's no way to determine how successful your marketing efforts have been. There are no truly objective metrics for marketing. The only appropriate metrics are those that you establish subjectively, based on your expectations and your history. You can look at your win rate, but what does it mean without goals? Is it high or low? Is 30 percent high or low? High or low as compared with what? Look at your revenue. It may be up, but is that necessarily the result of your marketing efforts, or necessarily an indication of success (it isn't if you can't deliver on your promises, or if you've sold your services too cheaply). Look at your backlog: It may have increased, but can marketing necessarily take credit for that?

You can look at your firm's overall performance in many ways and can apply many metrics to it. You can look at billability, total profit, profit per professional, total billings, total backlog, and others. But none of these provides an objective assessment of your marketing efforts. Marketing is an inherent component of the operations of your business. It doesn't work independently. As such, it's difficult or impossible to apply an objective set of metrics to your marketing success. All you can do is create a plan that includes goals and a process for achieving them, and then check back to see if it worked.

Revisit your marketing plan every year. Evaluate your goals and determine how successful you were. Make new goals for the coming year and develop a plan to achieve them. An annual process of reevaluating and revising your marketing plan keeps you on track and serves as an annual checkup on how well your marketing efforts are working. If you feel that you need a more frequent check-in, make brief quarterly goals, and reevaluate those every three months.

What If It Didn't Work? What Do You Do If You Didn't Meet Your Goals?

What if you made an annual marketing plan, with very clear goals, and at the end of the year it is apparent that those goals were not met. Let's say you had hoped to increase your academic work by 20 percent, and you didn't. Or you had hoped to increase your revenue by 10 percent, and you didn't. Is it just a dismal failure? What do you do now?

You can choose to interpret the failure in a number of ways and to adjust your strategy for the next year:

- *Your expectations were too high.* Your expectations were too ambitious and out of alignment with reality. For the next year, lower your expectations.

- *The plan was unrealistic.* The plan that you created to meet your goals was not sufficient to accomplish what you had hoped. In the next year, reevaluate and make a better plan.

- *There was an organizational breakdown.* The expectations were appropriate, and the plan was a good one, but there was an organizational breakdown that got in the way. Correct the organizational problem and try again.

- *This was somebody's fault.* Somebody was to blame for the goals not being met. An individual was entrusted with certain responsibility and did not work to expectations. Take the person out of the equation and try again.

- *External factors were to blame.* Maybe the economy collapsed, or one of your key markets dried up. Chalk it up to experience and make a new plan that takes into consideration what you've learned about the external environment.

When you evaluate the success of your marketing program each year, whether you succeeded or failed is not what is most important; most important is what you learned from the process and what you're going to do differently in the next year to improve. The fact that you follow a process of setting goals, trying to achieve them, and evaluating your success leads to qualitative improvement in itself. It is, by design, a process of continuing self-education and self-improvement. Just keep striving to accomplish your goals and you will necessarily get closer to achieving them.

Bibliography

General Marketing

Fisher, Roger, and William Ury. *Getting to Yes: Negotiating Agreement without Giving In.* New York: Houghton Mifflin Company, 1981.

Ries, Al, and Jack Trout. *Positioning: The Battle for Your Mind.* New York: McGraw-Hill, 2001.

Ries, Al, and Laura Ries. *The 22 Immutable Laws of Branding.* New York: HarperCollins Business (a division of HarperCollins Publishers), 1998.

Professional Services Marketing

Beckwith, Harry. *The Invisible Touch.* New York: Warner Books, 2000.

_____. *Selling the Invisible.* New York: Warner Books, 1997.

Berry, Leonard L., and A. Parasuraman. *Marketing Services: Competing through Quality.* New York: The Free Press (a division of Macmillan, Inc.), 1991.

Harding, Ford. *Rainmaking: The Professional's Guide to Attracting New Clients.* Avon, MA: Adams Media Corporation, 1994.

Kotler, Philip, Paul Bloom, and Thomas Hayes. *Marketing Professional Services.* New York: Prentice Hall Press, 2002.

Wilson, Aubrey. *The Marketing of Professional Services.* London: McGraw-Hill Book Company, 1972.

A/E/C Services Marketing

Coxe, Weld. *Marketing Architectural and Engineering Services.* New York: Van Nostrand Reinhold, 1971.

Flink, Robert, Esq. "Tips on Responding to RFPs," *OfficeInsight* (October 20, 2003): 7.

_____. "Responding to RFPs—Part 2: Specific Suggestions." *OfficeInsight* (October 27, 2003): 12–13.

Frost, Susan E. *Blueprint for Marketing: A Comprehensive Marketing Guide for Design Professionals.* Portland, OR: SEF Publications, 1993.

Greusel, David. *Architect's Essentials of Presentation Skills.* Hoboken, NJ: John Wiley & Sons, Inc., 2002.

Handley, Sally A., and Sharyn Yorio. *Charting Your Career Path: Opportunities for Professional Service Marketers in the 21st Century.* Alexandria, VA: The Society for Marketing Professional Services, 2001.

Handley, Sally A. "Evaluating the Marketing Effort: Define—Strategize—Measure," a white paper of The Marketing Partnership, April 1, 2003.

"How to Create an Annual Marketing Plan That Flies." *Design Firm Management & Administration Report* (January 1999): 1–12.

Jackson, Ellen, ed. *The Handbook for Marketing Professional Services.* Alexandria, VA: The Society for Marketing Professional Services, 1994.

Jones, Gerre. *How to Market Professional Design Services.* New York: McGraw-Hill, Inc., 1973.

Kliment, Stephen A. *Writing for Design Professionals: A Guide to Writing Successful Proposals, Letters, Brochures, Portfolios, Reports, Presentations, and Job Applications.* New York: W.W. Norton & Co., Inc., 1998.

Kolleeny, Jane, and Charles Linn, AIA. "Marketing: the Unsung Heroine of Successful Architectural Practice," *Architectural Record* (February 2001): 66–72.

_____. "Marketing: Building Your Firm's Incredible Marketing Machine," *Architectural Record* (March 2001): 76–84.

_____. "Marketing Today: Balancing People and Machines." *Architectural Record* (May 2001): 180–187.

Schrag, Dennis M. "A Closer Look: What Is Your Firm's Reputation on the Street? Research It," *SMPS Marketer* (February 2003): pp. 13–15.

Society for Marketing Professional Services. *Marketing Handbook for the Design & Construction Professional.* Los Angeles: BNi Publications, Inc., 2000.

Spaulding, Margaret, and William D'Elia. *Advanced Marketing Techniques for Architecture & Engineering Firms.* New York: McGraw-Hill Publishing Company, 1989.

Stasiowski, Frank A. *Architect's Essentials of Winning Proposals.* Hoboken, NJ: John Wiley & Sons, Inc., 2003.

Personal Marketing

Carnegie, Dale. *How to Win Friends and Influence People.* New York: Simon & Schuster, 1936.

Maister, David. *True Professionalism: The Courage to Care about Your People, Your Clients, and Your Career.* New York: Simon & Schuster, 1997.

Index